POLITICS

OF

CLINTON

AND

TRUMP

Max Vanguard
Author

TABLE OF CONTENTS

Max Vanguard

TRUMP

VS.

CLINTON

Book 1

INTRODUCTION

Chapter 1

The United States presidential election last year was the 58th ceremonial American presidential election, held on November 8, 2016. Math tells us that, when the voters reach election day, the campaign period was 597 days old. Mothers who are expecting a newborn when Ted Cruz announced his candidacy would be sporting a toddler at this time. It was a 20month relentless race to the top, months filled with ads, polls, debates and speeches. Not to mention the left and right issues that are thrown at the candidates. The 2016 Presidential election is truly one for the books, the number of controversies, and drama is like nothing that we have ever seen.

The turn of events during the final election week was as intense as it gets. The results turned out to be a surprise to many. Nonetheless, Americans remain to be hopeful about what's coming for the next four years.

Take a look back at some of the highlights of last year's Presidential campaign. We are pulling back the curtain on Trump and Clinton's respective presidential runs to uncover what actually happened behind the stage. From party loyalties to lawsuits, all the juicy stuff. All the stories you need to know about the presidential race is all here!

PRIMARY

Chapter 2

REPUBLICAN CANDIDATES

The Republican Party is one-half of the two major political party system in the U.S. they are generally referred to as the Grand Old Party or the GOP. The party is identified after republicanism, the principal value throughout the American Revolution.

The Republican Party's current philosophy is American conservatism, which contrasts with the Democrats' modern liberalism. The center beliefs of the Republican Party are focused on the idea that each person is responsible for their own place within society. The GOP believes in keeping the government should focus essentially on the state and community level, and not at a federal level.

For the 2016 Presidential Elections, the Republicans have lined up notable candidates:

John Ellis "Jeb" Bush Sr

John Ellis "Jeb" Bush Sr. was the former governer of Florida and the brother of former president George W. Bush as well as the son of president George Bush Senior.

Ben Carson

Ben Carson, a retired neurosurgeon, was born in Detroit, Michigan. Carson went to school at Yale University and went on to graduate from the University of Michigan Medical School. Carson has authored numerous books such as One Nation, Think Big, The Big Picture and You Have A Brain.

Carson was the youngest chief of pediatric neurosurgery in the United States when was just 33 years old.

John Kasich

Kasich sought the Republican nomination for president in 2000 and in 2016. Kasich was the former governor of Ohio and a former member of congress.

Jim Gilmore

James Stuart "Jim" Gilmore III a native Virginian was born October 6, 1949. From 1998 to 2002 he became the 68th Governor of Virginia.

He graduated from the University of Virginia in 1971 and then served as a counterintelligence agent in the U.S. Army. He served the public office as a county prosecutor, then as an Attorney General of Virginia, and later on elected as Governor of Virginia.

Gilmore was a candidate for the Republican nomination for President of the United States in the 2008 and 2016 elections.

Marco Rubio

Marco Antonio Rubio is an attorney politician born on May 28, 1971. He is a junior United States Senator from Florida and has previously served as Speaker of the Florida House of Representatives.

Rubio is a Cuban-American from Miami, with degrees from the University of Florida and the University of Miami School of Law. Back in 2000, he was elected to represent Florida's 111th district under the House of Representatives. In 2002 he was appointed as House Majority Leader. Afterward, in November 2006 he was elected as Speaker of the Florida House serving 2 years.
In 2008, Rubio began teaching at Florida International University and also establish his own law firm.

Rubio successfully ran for United States Senate in 2010. An April of 2015, he announced that he would seek higher office and run for President.

Donald Trump

Donald John Trump is an American entrepreneur born on June 14, 1946. He was born and raised in New York City and studied at Wharton School with a bachelor's degree in economics in 1968.

In 1971 he took over his family's construction and real estate company and renamed it The Trump Organization. From 1996 to 2015 he owned Miss

USA pageants and has also made cameo appearances in various series and films. He also hosted and co-produced a reality series The Apprentice.

Trump announced his candidacy for president as a Republican and quickly emerged as the front-runner for his party's nomination. His 2016 presidential campaign received unprecedented media coverage and international attention.

Additional Candidates included:
- Carly Fiorina, the former CEO of Hewlett-Packard
- Chris Christie the Governor of New Jersey
- Rand Paul the Senator from Kentucky
- Rick Santorum the former Senator from Pennsylvania
- Mike Huckabee the former governor of Arkansas
- George Pataki the former Governor of New York
- Lindsey Graham the Senator from South Carolina
- Bobby Jindal the Governor of Louisiana
- Scott Walker the Governor of Wisconsin
- Rick Perry the former governor of Texas

Max Vanguard

DEMOCRATIC CANDIDATES

The Democratic Party is the world's oldest active party, and is the other half of the two major political party in the United States, sharing its position with the Republicans.

Following its legacy back to Thomas Jefferson and James Madison's Democratic-Republican Party, now we have so-called modern-day Democratic Party which was established in 1828 by Andrew Jackson.

Today, the House Democratic assembly is formed largely of reformists and centrists, but there is still a minority of conservative Democrats present.

The party's ideology of modern liberalism that pushes equal social and economic rights. One of its goals is to implement government intervention on issues such as the country's economy. The party is after increasing social programs, aid labor unions, inexpensive college tuitions, reasonable health care and equal opportunity.

For the year 2016 National Elections, the Democratic party was able to put together distinguished names on the list:

Hillary Clinton

Hillary Clinton was born in Chicago, Illinois on October 26, 1947. As a child she lived in Park Ridge, a town in Illinois outside of Chicago. Hillary Diane Rodham Clinton was the first lady, a U.S. Senator and the former Secretary of State under President Obama from 2009 to 2013.

Hillary attended Wellesley College and graduated from Yale Law School. Subsequently, she served as a congressional legal counsel and moved to Arkansas where she married the former president Bill Clinton. She then served as a Senator from 2001 to 2009 and became the First Lady of the United States from 1993 to 2001. She ran for president in 2008 but lost the Democratic nomination to Barack Obama.

She was the Democratic Party's nominee for President of the United States in the 2016 election.

Bernie Sanders

Bernie was born and raised in the Brooklyn borough of New York on September 8, 1941. He was a graduate of University of Chicago in 1964. He settled in Vermont in 1968, and ran third-party campaigns for governor and U.S. senator in the 70s. In 1981 he won as an independent candidate for mayor of Burlington, Vermont.

In 1990 he was elected to represent the congressional district of Vermont in the U.S. House of Representatives. Bernie Sanders served as a congressman for 16 years before being elected to the U.S. Senate in 2006.

Sanders has built a reputation as a leading progressive voice on key issues such as campaign finance reform, corporate welfare, global warming, LGBT rights, parental leave, and universal healthcare.

Sanders announced his campaign for the Democratic presidential nomination on April 30, 2015.

Martin O'Malley

Martin Joseph O'Malley is an American politician born on January 18, 1963. He was the 61st Governor of Maryland from 2007 to 2015. Earlier he served as a city councilor for Baltimore from 1991 to 1999 and then later on elected as Mayor and stayed in office from 1999 to 2007

From 2011 to 2013 he was a chair of the Democratic Governors Association while being a governor of Maryland. He left public office in early 2015 and acted as a visiting professor at Johns Hopkins University's Carey Business School.

As governor, O'Malley is a known supporter of illegal immigrants and same-sex marriage in Maryland.

After seeking the Democratic Party nomination, he publicly announced his candidacy in the 2016 presidential election on May 30, 2015.

GREEN PARTY

The Green Party of the United States is a progressive political party operating inside the United States. They are often described as the eco-socialist party and is generally seen as the left-wing on the political spectrum.

Jill Stein was the Green Party candidate for the 2016 Presidential election. She received slightly more than 1% of the United States popular vote and collected none of the Electoral vote.

After the election was over Jill Stein did try and force a recount in the state of Wisconsin. Stein was not a contender but the election between Trump and Clinton in Wisconsin was too close to call. The recall would mean nothing to Stein, but with Trump declared the winner ion Wisconsin, the only person a recall could help would be Hillary. Stein also pushed for a recall in Michigan and Pennsylvania. Again Stein was not a contender but, perhaps was asking for a recount to try and help Hillary.

The Green political party is the country's fourth-largest party by the membership. The GPUS firmly believes and stands on Four Pillars, namely Ecological Wisdom, Social and Economic Justice, Grassroots Democracy, and Nonviolence and Peace. In general, it's members embrace environmentalism, non-hierarchical participatory democracy, social justice, and respect for diversity, peace, and nonviolence.

In its early years, the party was referred to as "Association of State Green Parties" until 2001 they decided to establish it as

"The Green Party United States", the party is largely composed of autonomous state or local based political entities with a weak national leadership structure that largely served to coordinate electoral activities.

During the 2000 presidential election, the party gained the public's attention when they won 2.7% vote with Ralph Nader and Winona LaDuke as their ticket. Nader was able to raised millions of dollars, which mobilized the leftist and seized national headlines with his anti-corporate campaign message. In return, he was accused of siphoning important votes away from Al Gore's campaign which then paved the way for George Bush's win for the presidency. Despite this, the party currently holds no federal or state-wide elected positions. Numerous Greens party members in the United States have positions such as the city mayors or town council members.

In 2016, the Green Party of the United States fought for equal access to the party's message for the American public to an increased coverage in the mainstream media and inclusion in the Presidential debates. The party also managed to tap 50% of independent Americans who are neither registered Democrats nor Republicans.

The party was impressed by Bernie Sander's performance and in April 2016 they aimed for Bernie Sanders and his supporters with the intention of exploring some of his ways and ideology and incorporating it within the Green Party of the United States.

LIBERTARIAN PARTY

Founded in 1971, the Libertarian Party is one of the longest serving and largest third parties of America.

Libertarians seek a middle ground between the liberal values and the conservative ones. The party strongly believes in total individual liberty and stands for pro-drug legalization, pro-choice, pro-gay marriage, pro-gun rights. The Libertarians are also for anti-government regulation of business, anti-minimum wage, anti-income tax, and pro-free trade. Generally, the Libertarians are after total economic freedom.

The Libertarian Party's (LP) general ideology revolves around the phrase "more freedom, less government and lower taxes" which is based on the traditional laissez-faire ("Hands off") philosophy.

For Years, the party has been divided between two aggressive factions, the purist libertarian group, and the moderate reform faction. The reform faction focuses mainly on popular issues such as drug decriminalization, gun rights and tax cuts as a way to attract a large number of voters. On the other hand, the devoted purist group is made up of strong anarchistic-libertarians who's advocacy is based on the principles of Ayn Rand. The purist and their allies faction firmly held control of the party from the late-1980s until the moderates took over and seized control at the 2006 national convention and completely change the party's original platform.

Currently, there are over 400 LP members holding various low-level government positions. In any given election year, the LP has since increased its nomination for the local and federal candidates more than any other US third party. However, since 1996 the Greens has shown an increase in the number of members and have maintained its following and garnering more and more media attention through the years.

CLINTON'S SUPERDELEGATES

United State's secretary of state and former first lady had a definite route towards the democratic party's presidential nomination. She's flowing in cash, running an efficient campaign team and facing just one rival, which is Senator Bernie Sanders.

The 2016 election should be easy compared to her last presidential run in 2008 when she went head to head with the historic candidacy of Barack Obama.

Bernie Sanders the primary challenger to Hillary Clinton did not make it easy for Hillary, in fact, Clinton struggled. At the New Hampshire primary, Sanders struck Clinton and got 151,000 votes compared to the 95,000 votes Clinton had. In other words, the woman widely recognized to be the Democrats' only possible presidential nominee just lost more than 60 percent of the vote to an outsider.

A political analyst said that there were two main reasons for Clinton's defeat. One is that New Hampshire has far fewer minority voters compared to other states, making it favorable for Sanders, who gets most of his support from the white people. It turns out that this was not just a New Hampshire issue. Several other states that did not have big cities with lots of minority voters decided to vote for

Sanders. For example Colorado, Utah, Wyoming, Montana, Minnesota, Indiana, Alaska and Maine were all states that Bernie Sanders won in the primary. Critics also pointed out that voters did not trust Clinton, and with Sanders' undeniable authenticity, the obvious choice would be the latter. In a conducted survey entitled "honesty and trustworthiness" among voters, Sanders led 92-6.

A week before the New Hampshire primary the campaign in Iowa was very close. Clinton had a razor-thin advantage over Sanders in Iowa. Nationally Senator Bernie Sanders has a dominant 56-42 percent lead.

Despite Sanders' lead and the 56,000 more vote Sanders received, Sanders actually ended up losing the Iowa caucus. This is because of the Democrats' complex nomination process, which many of his supporters claimed to be in favor of Clinton. Under this scheme, Sanders' big national lead is completely irrelevant.
The real battle between Clinton and Sanders was the fight for "delegates", who are assigned to them state-by-state. While some states award their delegates proportionally, based on each candidate's percentage of the vote, others simply grant all their delegates to whoever finishes first. The results of the Iowa caucus gave Clinton 23 delegates to Sanders 21 delegates.

In addition to these delegates, there is also a total of

712 so-called "superdelegates." These superdelegates are party leaders and chosen officials who supports whomever they like and ignore the voters. Amid the campaign, Clinton had around 90 percent of them in her corner.

The effect? Even after Iowa and New Hampshire, Clinton defeats Sanders in the one count that actually matters, with 90 percent of the delegates.

Earned Delegates
Clinton: 32
Sanders: 36

Super Delegates
Clinton: 362
Sanders: 8

Total Delegates
Clinton: 394
Sanders: 44

It is believed that Super delegates were made to give the people who controlled the party a huge say as to who the parties candidate will be. In this case due to the large amount of baggage and email that Clinton was carrying it make have helped Trump win the presidency. Clinton's only rival, Sanders wasn't complaining. He's looking for a repeat of Clinton's long, tough campaign against Barack Obama, in which she also posted an early lead among super delegates, then watched many of them defect as they realized Obama was going to be the nominee anyway.

Sanders said in a CBS interview. "If we continue to do well around the country, and if super delegates whose main interest in life is to make sure that we do not have a Republican in the White House and if they understand that I am the candidate who is best suited to defeat the Republican nominee, I think they will start coming over to us." The Democratic National Committee, which oversees the party's primaries, is also undermining the importance of superdelegates. If the party supports a candidate that the people don't want then the big loser is the party. The Democratic party did not fare well in this election. They did not win the presidency, they did not win back the Senate and the did not win back the House of Representatives.

It was clear that Hillary Clinton thought it was fare for her to have 90% of all these superdelegates. The party also seemed to agree. Patrice Taylor, Director of Party Affairs and Delegate Selection said, "Ultimately, each state's delegation is comprised of a diverse group of citizens like you and the Democratic leaders you have elected. This is a shameful policy where the leaders of the party think that what they think should be more important that what the voters think. The Republicans are not innocent in this behavior either. Both parties are wrong about this.

Regardless of how we look like at it, it is clear that Hillary Clinton already had a huge head start before anyone took notice. Clearly, the Clintons still had some control over the Democratic party apparatus. They used this control to influence to secure as many of the superdelegates as possible.

Hillary Clinton and Bernie Sanders were both fighting to try and reach a total of 2,383 delegates, which could be made up of primary delegates or superdelegates, to win the party's nomination.

In Democratic Primary, Clinton won 2,842 presidential primary delegates compared to Sanders 1,865 delegates. Of the 2,842 delegates Clinton received 571 superdelegates compared to sanders 45 superdelegates. If superdelegates had voted the opposite way (571 for Sanders and 45 for Clinton) then Sanders would have had 2391 and he would have won the Democratic nomination. This shows that the superdelegates was a large enough factor to decide this election.

COLORADO'S CONVENTION

The Republican part in Colorado has district and state conventions that tripped up Donald Trump. Cruz was able to navigate the primary election process to win 33 delegates to Trumps 1 delegate in Colorado.

Trump and many people were upset because it seems like state party rules were used to win the election. Clearly Cruz understood the rules and used them to his advantage. This turned out to be an important lesson for Trump. Trump realized that the election is won based on who has the most delegates. Nothing else matters. In the general election Trump and his election team concentrated on this fact.

The rules of the state were in fact changed in 2012, but this was not the reason for Trump's loss in Colorado. The rules only eliminated the meaningless straw polls that were performed.

However The Colorado Convention is not a simple process. Thousands of people descend on an stadium in Colorado Springs and then over 500 people will speak for about 20 seconds each. These people were trying to be chosen as one of one of the 37 Republican delegates. Some of the delegates are like Democratic superdelegates are selected before the process is open for the common convention voter.

The fascinating and backward way that Colorado selects their delegates has been going on for over 150 years. The election process in Colorado will probably be on the agenda of the new Republican party chairperson Ronna Romney McDaniel the niece of 2012 republican candidate: Mitt Romney.

Max Vanguard

SANDERS' FIGHT AGAINST CLINTON

Former Secretary of State Hillary Clinton's chief competitor for the nomination was Bernie Sanders. For months, Sanders and Clinton were often feisty rivals, as she progressed towards the Democratic nomination. Sanders continued to inspire a movement of millennials and had the Democratic party supported him at all then he might have been the president.

Sanders, the Vermont senator, went on to host several speeches, talking about key issues, such as universal healthcare, free higher education, and increasing the federal minimum wage. The camp of Bernie Sanders' actively directed its campaign over social media, the same platform which allowed candidate Sanders to fundraise around $200 million via small donations.

One of Sander's main advocacy and intention was to influence and encourage everybody to go to the polls and vote. Even after Clinton was declared the nominee base on the number of delegates and superdelegates she had collected, Bernie Sanders refused to concede.

And although Clinton has a clear lead on superdelegates, the Vermont senator said in an interview that he will compete for the position of Democratic nominee until the very last primary in

Washington DC. His words were "We are going to fight hard to win the primary in Washington, DC."

The superdelegates really hurt Bernie Sander's campaign. However, during this time, there were news reports that superdelegates, in reality, were not really committed as they claimed to be. Superdelegates can switch their votes at the convention or at any time before the convention. So it is correct to state that, superdelegate votes are not really Hillary's votes or Bernie's votes until votes until they are cast at the Democratic Convention.

Clinton's rival showed no sign of giving up as he sent out campaign emails to supporters and encourage them to vote and volunteer in anticipation of the final democratic primary held last June in Washington DC.

Senator Sanders was even labeled as sexist, to which he responded, "I don't think it is sexist, our focus right now is running and winning right here in California and the second point that I have made is that it is absolutely imperative that we defeat Donald Trump as a candidate for president of the United States. I believe that I am the stronger candidate."

He believed that beating Trump wasn't enough. In one of his interview, he mentioned "We've got to work tirelessly to make sure that Trump is not president but that is not good enough," he said. The Vermont senator said in a Democratic Party "political campaigns come and go, but political and social revolutions continue."

Even towards the end of the campaign period he showed no sign of wavering and told his supporters "we take our fight for social, economic, racial and environmental justice to Philadelphia," where the Democratic convention will take place. Indeed, even after Sander's national lead of 55,000 more votes against Clinton. At the final primary election on June 14, Clinton turned into the assumptive Democratic nominee.

Naturally, Senator Sanders' supporters were not thrilled. They blamed the superdelegates nomination effect and the democratic party's way and the process of nomination. Two petitions were made by a progressive activist group, demanding that superdelegates should follow the will of the voters, which had 322,000 signatures.

"This process is undemocratic and fundamentally unfair to Democratic primary voters," said Ilya Sheyman, the advocate group's executive director. Further Sheyman said, "Democracy only works when the votes of the people not the decision of a small number of elites, are what determines the outcome of elections" she also asserted, "Super delegates must stand with voters and honor the outcomes of primaries and caucuses held across the country. The party's base simply will not tolerate any anti-democratic efforts by super delegates to thwart the will of the people."

In spite of the fact that Sanders did not authoritatively endorse Clinton he promised to work with Hillary Clinton to beat Donald Trump

On July 22, 2016, emails exchanges coming from the Democratic National Committee, Debbie Wasserman Schultz, Luis Miranda and other high position Democrat party members that seems to be working directly against Sanders in an attempt to belittle and undermine his candidacy. Debbie Wasserman Schultz, resigned just prior to the Democratic Conversion on July 24th 2016. Schultz was succeeded by Donna Brazile, another Clinton loyalist who was additionally involved in the leaks and apologized to Sanders and his supporters.

THE OUTSIDERS

The primary post-debate poll of Iowa Republicans showed the rise of the outsiders. Notable candidates who assumed that voters would be influenced by their impressive record in public office were somewhat disappointed with the poll results.

It was evident that over 60% of the people from Iowa favored either one of the four political outsiders. According to the results, Cruz received 27.64%, Trump got 24.3%, Carson was able to secure 9.3%, and Fiorina received 1.9% in votes.

Cruz, positioned himself as an outsider from the U.S. Senate that believed deeply in his faith and the constitution of the United States.

Trump, for one, sets himself as a "developer" a sharp negotiator who takes care of business, whatever it might be, and who takes pleasure in pounding the "underdogs" of today's political class.

Carson brings to the table a mix of brilliance and calm quietude, whose accomplishments as a world-class specialist are genuinely impressive. His positivity rating of 79% among Iowa assembly voters did not come as a surprise.

With Fiorina, you got the expertise of a CEO of a

Fortune 500 company executive rather than a profession lawmaker.

THE DEBATES

Ever since the 1960 Presidential election debate that involved Richard Nixon and John F. Kennedy, historians had acknowledged that a televised debate had a profound effect on election results. The interest towards debates was increasingly valued.

The debates will not only help voters understand and hear the candidates address key issues prior elections, but they will also have a clear knowledge of who they want to support in the running. All thanks to the beauty of a Democratic type of government.

Here is what transpired during the 3 Presidential debates.
First Presidential Debate

First Presidential Debate
Donald Trump's self-ruling method has gone out of control in the first presidential debate as he was constrained on the defensive during the encounter with Hillary Clinton.

Instigated by moderator Lester Holt and hounded by Clinton, the Republican nominee angrily defended his record against attacks of racism, sexism and tax evasion for much of the debate held at Hofstra University, just outside New York.

Trump was able to call out Clinton on issues such as trade and her political record. These issues usually helped Trump draw level in the polls but never to a commanding lead. This move made the businessman looked under-prepared and thin-skinned as he choked his way through the debate. "It's all words, it's all sound bites," he answered after a one-sided exchange, stating that Hillary Clinton was a "typical politician: all talk, no action".

But the Democratic nominee was quick to rebut on Trump's nomadic responses and the seemingly lack of focus on the on-going debate meeting. Clinton said, "Words matter when you run for president, and they really do matter when you are president," Then went on to say, "I think Donald just criticized me for preparing for this debate. And yes I did. You know what else I did? I prepared to be president," There was a moment where Clinton attacked Trump for racism because he questioned Barack Obama's citizenship. Hillary added, "He has a long record of engaging in racist behavior. And the birther lie was a very hurtful one." Clinton also attempted to implicate that Trump was, "stiffing thousands" of contractors by declaring bankruptcy during a point in his career as a businessman. In a closing argument, Clinton pointed out Trump's record of sexism, and added that Trump had refered to women as pigs and slobs. Further see asserted that in one case, called he insulted a beauty contestant by calling her "Miss Housekeeping".

Trump then attacked Clinton's capability as president in simple terms. He said, "She doesn't have the look and she doesn't have the stamina," he said. "I've been all over the place. You decided to stay home," he added.

Clinton responded by stating her accomplishment of visiting 112 countries in her 4-year term as the secretary of state. Clinton also fired back saying "When Donald Trump spends 11 hours testifying in front of a congressional committee, he can talk to me about stamina."

This backfire against Trump and worked in favor of Clinton. The questions of stamina and temperament were a testament that Trump indeed lack focus and concentration during the uninterrupted debate, which was his first one-on-one appearance on a political debate stage.

Immediately after the debate, Trump took to the media spin room to defend his performance. Boris Epsheteyn, Trump's campaign spokesman, blamed the moderator, saying "Lester Holt interrupted Mr. Trump more. He followed up with Mr. Trump more. He was much harder on Mr. Trump."

Meanwhile, Clinton's campaign team declared that the debate had highlighted that Trump was both "unhinged and unfit to be president" – but at the same time, they were cautious to sustain expectations.

In an interview, John Podesta, the Clinton campaign chairman, said, "He came in unprepared and what we saw was kind of a meltdown."

Clinton's campaign manager Robby Mook, cannot let the debate pass without commenting, so this is what he had to say "We'll have to see how the voters judge this." He added, "But I think the consensus of this entire debate was that Secretary Clinton was the only one on that stage prepared to be president, and I think the totality of the debate proved how deeply unfit he was."

Before the debate, Clinton spent the afternoon preparing with her campaign aides at Garden City Hotel. Meanwhile, Trump attended and participated in a pre-debate walk-through at Hofstra University.

Afterward, while Trump was taped hastily escaping in his car, Clinton told supporters at a debate watch party to keep supporting, telling them: "You saw tonight how high the stakes are."

Early on in the debate, Trump said to Clinton "Is that OK? I want you to be happy. It's very important to me," He appeared to be trying to keep everything under control and not be aggressive.

It was noticeable that during the debate Trump was

sniffing heavily and was having a nasal congestion problem. He quickly grew agitated, and he repeatedly interrupted Clinton.

Trump went after Clinton's support of her husband, Bill Clinton because when Bill was preseident he has signed into law the North America Free Trade Agreement (NAFTA) in the 1990s. Trump thought it was a bad deal for American workers. The effects of NAFTA, after it was signed into law by Bill Clinton, were the loss of 700,000 American jobs that moved to Mexico. NAFTA also helped Employeers by putting more pressure on American workers to accept lower pay. The Mexican agricultural worker was also displaced which resulted in more illegal immigrants in the United states. NAFTA was also the framework which helped drive additional agreements which would help give China access to the US markets by allowing big american corporations access to invest in China.

Clinton immediately hit Trump, because of the $14 million that he got from his father through a series of loans. His father Fred Trump, a successful real estate developer helped fund the younger Trump's effort to remodel the Grand Hyatt hotel in Manhattan and also helped him with his political connections. Trump was quick, and fired back "it was only a small loan." Trump was able to come back and jabbed Clinton for previously promoting the Trans-Pacific Partnership, the notable 12-

nation trade pact brokered under the Obama administration. When Clinton was trying to answer that she no longer supports the agreement, Trump meddled with the phrases "Is it President Obama's fault?"

Clinton smiled and said, "Donald, I know you live in your own reality." Lester Holt, the debate's mediator was unmistakably experiencing considerable difficulties to stay on theme as the two nominees exchange points that faltered amongst their personal life. He particularly said that Trump was in reality, a test to control given his forceful impulse that did not necessarily address the question being asked.

The two nominees began exchanging fiery allegations. Clinton began with Trump's tax issues as when he was a businessman. Trump was quick to pledged to release his tax returns when the secretary of state released the 33,000 emails deleted from her private home server.

Clinton fired back and continued to press all the hypothetical reasons why Trump was not releasing his tax returns. Clinton stated "perhaps Trump was not as rich as he says he is, not as charitable as he says he is" and the former first lady even implied that the businessman turned politician did not pay taxes for years. Trump responded "that makes me smart" and Clinton continued, "I think he is probably not all that enthusiastic about having the rest of the country see because it must be something really important, even terrible that he is trying to hide."

While it is certainly true that Trump may not have paid taxes in years, this was due to him suffering nearly a billion dollar loss many years ago. The IRS allows losses to be written off against gains. In some sense Clinton's argument was silly because was Clinton suggesting that Trump should pay more tax then he was legally required to pay? Nobody does. If people want to give more they don't give to the United States government. They give to a charity of their choice.

After the debate, Jason Miller, Trump's senior communications adviser, avoided interrogations from reporters on whether the Republican nominee has settled his income taxes, Miller's reaction was "of course he pays taxes" and insisted that "he has paid taxes at every level."

Trump was also put on the hot seat for his past support of the Iraq war by both Clinton and the debate moderator. The Republican nominee stood by his claim that he did not support the war.

On climate change, Trump denied Clinton's claim that, "Donald thinks climate change is a hoax by the Chinese." The Republican nominee was quick to answer and said "I did not say that," however, there was an evidence of Trump's tweet in

November 2012 that read, "The concept of global warming was created by and for the Chinese in order to make US manufacturing non-competitive." And there were a couple of interviews where he clearly and repeatedly refers to global warming as "a hoax". Global warming to this day is not proven. Climate Change is real, but what causes the climate change is not known. The difference between Global Warming and Climate change is that Global Warming refers to the warming of the earth as being caused by humans, while climate change is the natural change in earth temperature over the years. For example between 1100 AD and 1200 AD the world temperature was warmer than it was today according to an IPCC report in 1990. Further if you go back in time we know there were ice ages where the planet got very cold, then the planet warmed and the glaciers disappeared. This cycle repeat several times. Something caused the temperature changes when humans were not around. The question is what is that cause. Some scientists say Sun spot activity is the cause but there is no definitive proof. So while Climate change is real, global warming may be a "hoax".

Even with the Republican nominee's rugged performance, where he repeatedly contradicted himself, Trump had already endured a number of controversies. On the night of the first debate, he didn't change his approach.

After the first Presidential debate, the only thing

left to ponder is how the polls will react after it has already tightened in recent days before the debate.

Second Presidential Debate

A shaken but challenging Republican candidate Donald Trump tried at the second debate to move past the video of him talking about touching women's genitalia. The release of this video had sent Trump's presidential campaign into a plunge.

Trump define his comments as "locker room talk," and immediately issued a dismissive apology, and when pushed by Anderson Cooper, Trump claimed he never kissed or fumbled women without their consent, and tried to change the topic as quickly as possible.

Trump accused Clinton of tainting women who've accused her husband of assault and Trump added that Clinton should be "ashamed" for even addressing his comments. In a notable remark, Trump told his rival that if he's elected, "you'd be in jail" he pledged to designate a prosecutor to investigate Clinton's email controversy.

Trump's overall performance, directing the same fury lifted his outsider bid all the way to the GOP nomination, may have been the key to subduing a large number of his supporters.

After taking the stage, both nominees said a brisk

hello but bypassed the usual traditional handshake. Clinton then cut to the chase and went on with her strategy that directed at letting Trump hang himself. Clinton avoided interrupting Trump's answers, and while she had sharp words to say about her opponent's video comments — the former first lady bolsters Trump's unsuitability for office.

"This is who Donald Trump is," Clinton had this to say for his recorded comments while pointing to its consistency with insulting remarks he's made public during a campaign about Muslims, Hispanics, African-Americans, and POWs. "And the question for us, the question our country must answer is that this is not who we are." Soon after, in response to Trump nagging about her deleted emails, Clinton finally hit back with: "OK, Donald. I know you're into big diversion tonight, anything to avoid talking about your campaign and the way it's exploding and the way Republicans are leaving you."

In general for the second debate, Clinton projected a poker face, showing disinterest and occasional musing as Trump continued on the attack. And at one point Trump had nothing to say but "Believe me, she has tremendous hate in her heart."

The downside of the first and second debate was that much of the time went to the conflict and counter-conflict over Trump's taped comments and the Clintons' own history. Top concerns and issues like creating more jobs were left with limited attention. However, there was a point in the debate where economic exchange was discussed and revolved around the candidate's respective tax plans.

When asked what's their take on the tax code to ensure that the wealthiest Americans pay their share, Trump responded first by discussing the capital gains treatment of carried interest is to blame, and he'd eliminate this saying. "One of the greatest provisions for people like me, to be honest with you," The Republican pledge for tax cuts for corporations of all sizes and a "big league" cut for the middle class. Being true to his character he warned Clinton saying "raise your taxes really high." and use this argument and press that Clinton represents the status quo and that she accomplishing nothing over her 30 years in public service.

Clinton answered by dismissing Trump's answer in its totality as untrue following a statement "I'm sorry I have to keep saying this, but he lives in an alternative reality."

Clinton stated, seeing the irony of quarreling over the code with a nominee who has refrained from paying his income tax for about two decades.

She went on to call Trump's plan a gift to the rich, "more than the Bush tax cuts by at least a factor of two." On the other hand, she said she'd offer a tax shield to anybody acquiring under $250,000 from any hikes while pushing the Buffett Rule for anybody gaining over $1 million and an additional charge on revenues above $5 million.

This exchange gave a chance for the moderators to follow up with Trump about his alleged nonpayment. And he appeared to acknowledge it. When asked if he used the $916 million loss he recorded in 1996 to offset paying income taxes in subsequent years. Trump confirmed this. As a fact check it is legal to do this and anyone with loss in the stock market, real estate or other areas of investment is allowed to do this. The IRS does limit how much one can recover per year. So Trump would only be able to recover a small portion of his loss each year. Trump also stated that the same write off was taken by Clinton's top donors.

The repeated dismal encounter at least ended on a lighter note. Prompted by the last audience questioner asking to name something admirable about the opposition, Clinton referred to Trump's children as wealth to him while Trump admired Clinton's determination. For a moment in the debate, it felt like a genuine yet careful exchange of goodwill. The Second Presidential debate then concluded by a handshake.

Third Presidential Debate

The third Presidential debate happened in Vegas, and this time what happened in Vegas won't stay in Vegas. Hillary Clinton and Donald Trump took part in their final TV debate before November's presidential election.

It was the last chance for Hilary Clinton and Donald Trump to take advantage of a national stage and make some impressive moments and statements for the voters.

Prior to the third Debate Donald Trump meet with several women who had accused Bill Clinton, Hillary's husband, of rape at a press conference. The women included Paula Jones, Kathleen Wiley and Juanita Broaddrick as well as others. Kathy Shelton, a women had been raped many years ago. Hillary Clinton was the lawyer who defended the accused rapist and got her client off as not guilty and then laughed about it. Trump supported these women to show that he did care about women and because it showed that Hillary had been an enabler for Bill Clinton's womanizing ways for decades.

The Republican nominee's performance in the first two debates came with a blow. Allegations of sexual assault led to a steep drop in Trump's state polls.

Trump displayed political progress and decided to invite Pat Smith, a Benghazi victim's mother, and

Malik Obama, Barack's estranged half-brother. He also mentioned in a repeated instance that elections will be rigged.

Clinton started the final debate with a clear lead but had to keep her head above water because of WikiLeaks's release of John Podesta's hacked emails. Podesta was the chairman of Hilary Clinton's presidential election campaign. Analysts said that the third debate could be the answer to resolving her credibility issues. It was also a missed opportunity for the Democratic nominee to offer herself as a viable option to Republicans who have been jumping off Trump's bandwagon and to maybe expand the Democratic map and enter red states like Arizona and Georgia.

Fox News' Chris Wallace was the chosen moderator for the final debate, this is the first time an anchor from the network has been selected to oversee a general election debate. Wallace was expected to be tough and unforgiving to both nominees. Wallace prepared six 15-minute segments, these segment included topics of immigration, debt and entitlements, Supreme Court, the economy, foreign hot spots, and most importantly eligibility to be president.

On the first debate segment, one of Wallace's topic was late-term abortions, Trump used this instance to accuse Clinton of supporting a practice in which "in the ninth month you can ... rip the baby out of the womb of the mother just prior to the birth of the baby."

Trump has made it clear from the start of his campaign that he abhors immigrants, saying: "They're bringing drugs. They're bringing crime. They're rapists." From more than a year into his campaign, Trump has not changed his stand on the issue, doubling down on the assumption that immigrants are criminals during the debate.

During the debate, Clinton got the chance to address the WikiLeaks hack by questioning Trump's active support of Russian espionage against "the American people." Which Trump replied, "Now we can talk about Putin. I don't know Putin. He said nice things about me. If we got along well, that would be good."

When Trump challenged whether the election espionage was linked to Russia, Clinton fired back and said, "He'd rather believe Vladimir Putin than the military and civilian intelligence professionals who are sworn to protect us." Trump answered, "She doesn't like Putin because Putin has outsmarted her at every step of the way." Again, Trump emphasized that Putin "is not my best friend." And added, "But if the United States got along with Russia, it wouldn't be so bad."

The debate moderator, Wallace brought up Trump's pessimist cries about what he describe as a rigged election. Wallace stated that Kellyanne Conway, Trump's campaign manager, Trump's running mate, and Trump's daughter have agreed to recognize the poll results. To which Trump's answer was "I will tell you at the time, but I will keep you in suspense." Clinton was quick to respond to Trump's remark, saying: "This is horrifying. Let's be clear about what he is saying and what that means. He is taking down our democracy." Clinton added that that statement is a remarkable admission and a direct challenge to the American democratic system suggested by a Republican nominee. This statement would come back to haunt Hillary after the election when it was she, not Trump who questioned the elections. There were riots in the streets and Hillary was trying joining a recount effort by the Green party in Wisconsin, Michigan and Pennsylvania. This was one of the big faults that been brought up during the election. Hillary had a public position on an issue, while have a different private opinion on the same issue. Here was an example where Hillary publicly stated that the American Democracy was at risk if the losing candidate did not accept the results. But when she lost, her private position of wanting to win took over.

The process of picking a running mate is often called the "veepstakes." The term suggests that the process is a game, and it is significant to make the right decision. According to history, nine vice presidents have become president due to the death or resignation of the president, but promising vice presidential candidates tend to receive less criticism than federal judges and cabinet picks.

Presidential candidates may decide on their running mates for many reasons. Some believe expand their appeal and improve their chances in the election by choosing a running mate very distinct from themselves. Others choose a running mate based on geography, to win over areas where support may be limited. And some concentrate on selecting an individual who would be a capable vice president or president.

Democratic Party Democratic vice presidential candidate Tim Kaine. A US junior senator who served as mayor of Richmond from 1998 to 2001 and a governor of Virginia from 2006 to 2010. Kaine also acted as the chair of the Democratic National Committee from 2009 to 2011.

Three days before the start of the Republican National Convention, Republican presidential nominee Donald Trump announced on social media that he had selected Indiana Gov. Mike Pence as his running mate. And on July 16, 2016, Trump formally introduce Pence as his "partner" in the race at a news conference in New York City.

Pence, at age 57, is the governor of Indiana. He describes himself as "a Christian, a conservative, and a Republican, in that order." Pence earlier served in the United States House of Representatives representing Indiana's 2nd Congressional District from 2001 to 2013.

A vice presidential debate took place on October 4, 2016, at Longwood University in Farmville, Virginia. It was considered to be the only vice presidential debate of the 2016 general election season.

Participants in the vice presidential debate included Tim Kaine and Mike Pence.

The Commission on Presidential Debates is a nonpartisan organization who takes charge and oversees the general election debates. The commission announced that Libertarian vice presidential nominee Bill Weld, and Green Party vice presidential nominee Ajamu Baraka, were not invited to attend the debate. The CPD required the nominee to have a 15 percent or higher polling average in order to be invited to the debate. During the time, the Libertarian Party bet was polling at 8.4 percent in the polls used by the CPD. And the

Green Party's Baraka registered only a 3.2 percent rating. The two failed to satisfy the CPD's criteria for inclusion. The commission is left with a Kaine versus Pence match.

Wisconsin Gov. Scott Walker helped Pence prepare by playing the role of Kaine on mock debate sessions. On the Democratic side, D.C. attorney Bob Barnett played the role of Pence during Kaine's mock debate sessions. Barnett also helped Clinton with debate prep in the 2016 Democratic primaries by playing as Vermont Sen. Bernie Sanders.

Both candidates, Indiana Governor Mike Pence and Virginia Senator Tim Kaine, spent most of the debate talking about Trump and Clinton the two main candidates for president. They also attacked the policy proposals of the rival's campaign.

The rules of the debate allowed Pence and Kaine to talk to one another during the 90-minute-long event. But this lead to a mush up, the two often talked at the same time or interrupt while the other was speaking.

Pence criticized Clinton's policies during her time as secretary of state for the current situation in the Middle East. He said her policies only allowed the Islamic State group to grow in strength and double in numbers. Pence also called Clinton over what he called a "newly emboldened Russia."

Kaine, on the other hand, stated that the Republican's Trump cares about himself before anyone else. And he challenged Pence and claimed that Trump had business connections with Russia that he "refuses to disclose."
Both vice presidential candidates agree that action should be taken to protect civilians in northern Syria. Pence suggested the creation of a no-fly zone in the area. He said that if Russia is connected to the attacks on the Syrian city of Aleppo, then the United States forces should attack Syrian military targets. The two men also settled on the issue of the increasing need for criminal justice reforms.

During the debate, Pence praise Trump's character as a businessman who operated many successful businesses and has created thousands of jobs. Kaine however, was quick to counter by repeatedly demanded that Trump releases his tax records. Many Democrats believe that the business mogul has not paid federal taxes for years.

On the issue of tax cuts, Kaine said Trump's plan to cut taxes would only help rich people and eventually lead to a recession. Pence was firm and said that Clinton's economic plan would clearly increase taxes and government spending.
Kaine also scrutinized Trump for his stand that more countries should have nuclear weapons. Pence claimed that more nuclear weapons would make us safer.

When the debate was done, political analyst said they were pleased that the both the vice presidential candidate talked generally about politics, and not of personal nature.

John Hudak said, "It stands in contrast to the first presidential debate, which was very personally oriented, very focused on scandals, very focused on guttural politics, and not so much about what the future of America is going to look like."
Lisa Spies who worked for Pence when he served in the U.S. Congress, said: "We got details, we got facts, we got numbers." Spies also noted, "During the presidential debate, we had adjectives and adverbs, and we had insults thrown at each other, and name-calling at each other. Tonight, even though there were interruptions, they were both stating what their policies would be."

Supporters of the two candidates accused the other side of running a sloppy campaign. John Podesta, the chairman of Hillary Clinton's drive for the presidency, criticized Donald Trump. Podesta in a statement said, "I think he has run an insult-driven campaign and I think that what Tim Kaine did tonight was to challenge Mike Pence to try to defend the hateful campaign."

Jeb Hensarling a known Trump supporter said, "It's clear that all the name-calling was coming from Tim Kaine. I mean, some of his charges were so over the top. It's something I would expect to see in a grocery store tabloid. I just think he lost credibility with the American people. He was just lodging charge after charge after charge."

Hillary Clinton's Private Emails

Even with the State Department's clearing thousands of pages of Hilary's e-mail, controversy still encompasses Hillary's use of a private e-mail server over allotted departmental servers amid her time as Secretary of State. The secretary of state insisted that the issue was only used by her detractors, some are still very suspicious that Clinton may have deleted e-mails that belong in the public domain. Hillary has admitted to deleting a few e-mails that she believe was personal.

This scandal is one that numerous members of the GOP will need to use to bring doubt upon Clinton as having purposely concealed data from the American people. Whether it'll stick is completely far from being obviously true, but do not expect this issue to die soon because the matter will come up over and over until the end of the decision.

Hillary Clinton decided prior to set up a private email computer server prior to her taking the job as Secretary of State. This was against government policy. It would be illegal for her to receive or send classified documents. This is not simple thing to do. First you have buy the computer system, then you need get the system configured and finally you have to have someone maintain the server. Any private citizen is allowed to set up a private email server. The issue that one runs into is when you work for government and you deal with classified information, then when the documents and emails sit on the server which is unsecured, you are breaking the law.

Hillary did not use a standard state department email address that ended with '@state.gov,' instead she used '@ClintonEmail.com. The physical server was kept in her house in Chappaqua, New York.

Initially when Clinton started to travel as secretary of state she used a blackberry phone which was connecting to her server using an unencrypted protocol. She should have been using Encryption software on her phone to have her emails encrypted. Communication between a phone and an email server will be routed by several servers on internet. Each machine that the message passes through is called a hop. In would not be uncommon for a message to go through 20 or more hops. At each one of these hops and even in between these hops a foreign government or a hacker can copy the message that is being sent or received. When the data is encrypted the party that intercepts the message cannot read it. But if the data is unencrypted then they can read the message just like a Microsoft Word document on your computer.

On July 5th 2016, Jim Comey, the director of the FBI said that Hillary was extremely careless in her handling highly sensitive classified information. Jim Comey went on to say that no reasonable prosecutor would bring such a case. The second statement by Comey is strange since he clearly indicated that she mishandled top secret classified documents. Being ignorant is not an excuse. If you think it is then just try not paying your income taxes and property taxes and see if your assets are not seized and your house foreclosed on.

Jim Comey on July 7th 2016 appeared before congress and was questioned by Trey Gowdy (Republican from South Carolina). Below is a transcript that shows that Hill

Gowdy asked, "Secretary Clinton Stated that she never received classified email over her private server. Is that true?"

Comey responded, "Our Investigation found that there was classified information sent."

Gowdy asked, "Secretary Clinton said there was not marked classified on her emails either sent or received. Was that true?"

Comey responded, "That is not true. There were a small number of portion markings on I think 3 of the documents."

Gowdy asked, "Secretary Clinton said I did not send any classified material to anyone on my email.

There is no classified material. Was that true?"

Comey replied, "No there was classified material emailed."

Gowdy continued with, "Secretary Clinton said she used just one device. Was that true?"

Comey replied, "She used multiple devices during her 4 years as secretary of state."

Gowdy then asked, "Secretary Clinton said all work related emails were returned to the state department. Was that true?"

Comey replied, "No we found work related emails. Thousands that were not returned."

Gowdy continue with, "Secretary Clinton stated that neither she nor anyone else deleted emails from her personal account. Was that true?"

Comey answered, "That is a harder one to answer. We found traces of work related emails. On devices or in slack space. Whether they were deleted or when a server was changed out something happened to them. There is no doubt that work related emails were removed electronically from the email system."

Gowdy asked, "Secretary Clinton said her lawyers read every one of her emails and were overly inclusive. Did the lawyers read the email content individually?"

Comey quickly replied, "No"

Gowdy continued to question why Comey did not use these false exculpatory statements against Hillary Clinton and why a common soldier from the military that emailed classified pictures to himself would be discharged from the Military but Hillary Clinton would get a pass and be allowed to be elected to commander in chief.

Hillary Clinton's Benghazi Failure

On September 11th 2012 United States government facilities in Benghazi Libya were attacked by Islamic forces from a group know to the United States as Ansar al-Sharia. The result of the attack left four Americans dead, it was under Hillary Clinton's term as the Secretary of State when it happened.

Hillary told her daughter that a terrorist group was responsible for the attack, however what Hillary and the Obama administration told the public was that the attack was a spontaneous attack that was cause by a Youtube.com video:

https://www.youtube.com/watch?v=kovTkWnasYk

Hillary later tried to explain why she had two

position.   She claimed that the information was changing by the hour and it was complicated.

But 24 hours after the attack Hillary Clinton told Hesham Kandil, the Egyptian Prime Minister, that the Benghazi attack, "had nothing to do with the film."   Clinton also stated that "it was a planned attack – not a protest."

This would seem to point to Clinton and/or the Obama administration lying about what happened. Obama at the time was worried about being re-elected.   Thus news about terrorists was unacceptable since The Obama Administration was saying terrorism is on the run.

What is strange is if you have American's in serious trouble then the logical conclusion that a rational person, that does not have a secret agenda, would be to just send help. So why didn't Hillary and the Obama administration just send the military to help? They had no way of knowing how long the compound at Benghazi could hold out.   Or why didn't they ask one our allies in the area to help? Or did they not really want to send help?

Why was Ambassador Stevens in Benghazi in the first place? Benghazi is not the capital of Libya. What was he doing there? Some have speculated that he was helping the Obama administration with gun running for Libyan jihadists fighting Moammar Gadhafi, the dictator of Libya. If this were the case then letting Stevens die would tie-up loose ends. Did Clinton and Obama support sending arms to terrorists in Libya and later Syria? If this were true would they ever want this to be public knowledge? Of course many simply believe that this is impossible the president would never provide guns to terrorists or people that could cause harm to Americans or other civilians. Right? Well of course the answer wrong. President Obama already did this in the United States of American when he authorized "Operation Fast and Furious." Fast and Furious was an operation that was supposed to help the United States destroy drug cartels that were doing "illegal drug business" within the United States. The operation was a complete failure. This operation ended up putting two-thousand weapons in the hands of the drug dealers so that the government could supposedly trace the guns. The weapons were used by drug lords to kill hundreds of Mexicans and a United States Border Agent. Guns From Obama's Fast and Furious program also were linked to Drug kingpin Joaquin "El Chapo" Guzman. He was found to have a .50-caliber rifle from the Fast and Furious which could be used to shoot down a helicopter. Obama and the White House that Hillary was a part of has attempted several times to assert executive privilege to prevent Congress from seeing documents related to Fast and Furious.

So one can clearly see that the Obama administration had no trouble giving out guns to drug lords. So It is not the big a leap to believe that

Hillary and Obama were giving out guns to terrorist to try to get them to take down the Libyan dictator Gadhafi. Although Gadhafi had become less of threat in his old age and had given up materials for his Nuclear and weapons of mass destruction program in 2003 and Libya had signed the Nuclear Non-Proliferation Treaty (NPT). This brings up the question of the judgment of Hillary and Obama since Gadhafi was really not a threat to the United States. Thus what we see is Hillary and Obama trying to bring about change in the Middle East, but ending up allowing Terrorism to grow in Libya, Syria, IRAQ and Yemen. While at the same time appeasing the Terrorist State IRAN by sending millions of dollars in cash and signing an agreement with IRAN that allows them to build nuclear weapons.

There were hundreds of requests for additional security from Ambassador Chris Stevens that were sent by Stevens several days before the attack on Benghazi even started. All the requests were ignored by Hillary and the State department. Why was Hillary surprised when an attack occurred on 9/11?

There are a lot of questions and no answers. This in itself speaks to trustworthiness of Hillary Clinton. She and the Obama administration were not disclosing what they were doing. And the result was the Middle East became very unstable, Leaders in Egypt, Libya, Syria, Yemen and IRAQ were either toppled or cornered. The destabilization of all these countries has cause a massive refugee problem and the rise of Al-Qaeda, a large terrorist organization that now exists in multiple countries.

Ted Cruz's Curiosity on Government Shutdown

Congressman Ted Cruz had an extensive turn in the administration shut down of 2013, making a line in the sand opposite President Obama. It was a move that angered many, incorporating legislators in his own party. Castigate for forcing the issue without having no plan to escape the shutdown, numerous GOP representatives lay the fault of the failure decisively at Cruz's feet.

While that could be subdued, Cruz kept on using an administration shut down as a strategy, totally overlooking that the last shutdown brought about wide disappointment with the Republican party. Cruz should understand that while his base may not really like the administration they have, they would prefer essentially not to see everything close down.

Carly Fiorina's Blunders as a CEO

While asserting your experience as a CEO as a positive, you'll likewise need to acknowledge the negatives, and Carly Fiorina has a noteworthy screw up on her resume - a forced resignation as CEO of Hewlett-Packard Company. This came as an immediate consequence of her driving a merger with Compaq against overwhelming restriction from half of the shareholders. Her progressions inside likewise infuriated many majority representatives.

The outcome? A decrease in stock costs that was far more honed than whatever is left of the tech world being dinged by the blasting of the tech bubble. Keeping in mind there was an increase in income, it was totally offset by the expansion owing debtors collected during her time. When she was constrained out of HP, numerous representatives cheered, and HP's stock bounced extensively, including $3 billion dollars in one day.

Sanders's Separation from the Democratic Party

For all practical purposes, Bernie Sanders is an independent. As far as the party alliance goes, he's running as a Democrat particularly for across the country vote access and to push the debate of left-wing legislative issues.

Nonetheless, among the more moderate Democrats, they may not consider Sanders to be a genuine member of the party and not a serious probability for selection. In the event that people questioning his legitimacy, he will be unable to change the debate as much as he'd like, to state nothing of an actual designation.

Ted Cruz Citizenship

To the disarray of civics students throughout, Ted Cruz was conceived in Canada, however, numerous law experts trust it won't block him from running for the administration. Be that as it may, it's the kind of story that, in the age where birthers still claim Obama is not a rightful president because of his birth issues, an issue that will not go away.

Regardless of the possibility that the legitimacy issue disappears, there's truly no getting around jokes about his birth home. Such subjects can divert from Cruz's policy claims, and turn a serious running into a gag line at the comedy bar.

TRUMP VERSUS MEGAN KELLY

The famed story of Fox News host Megyn Kelly and Republican nominee Donald Trump and created a bang during the Republican Party primaries that seemed to have died down in the past months.

The fight between Trump and Kelly started Aug. 6, 2015, at the first Republican presidential debate, when the two had a controversial back-and-forth.

In the opening round of questions, the host of The Kelly File went directly after the Republican front runner and poll leader, business billionaire Donald Trump.

In a question directed at Trump, Kelly said, "Mr. Trump, one of the things people love about you is you speak your mind and you don't use a politician's filter," she said. "However, that is not without its downsides, in particular, when it comes to women. You've called women you don't like, 'fat pigs,' 'dogs,' slobs, and disgusting animals."

Trump inserted a one-liner: "Only Rosie O'Donnell."

Kelly pushed on. "No, it wasn't," she said. "Your Twitter account has several disparaging comments about women's looks. You once told a contestant on Celebrity Apprentice it would be a pretty picture to see her on her knees. Does that sound to you like the temperament of a man we should elect as president, and how will you answer the charge from Hillary Clinton, who was likely to be the Democratic nominee, that you are part of the war on women?"

Trump countered by claiming that "the big problem this country has is being politically correct." He added "Frankly, what I say, and oftentimes it's fun, it's kidding," he said. "We have a good time. What I say is what I say. And honestly Megyn, if you don't like it, I'm sorry."

Another question that stood out to Trump was Kelly asking him "Mr. Trump, in 1999, you said you were, quote, 'very pro-choice.' Even supporting partial-birth abortion. You favored an assault weapons ban as well. In 2004, you said in most cases you identified as a Democrat. Even in this campaign, your critics say you often sound more like a Democrat than a Republican, calling several of your opponents on the stage things like 'clowns' and 'puppets.' When did you actually become a Republican?" Trump find this question out of bounds and offensive to which he feels Kelly should issue an apology.

After the debate, Trump tweeted "Wow, @megynkelly really bombed tonight. People are going wild on twitter! Funny to watch."

Despite Clinton's lead in polls, it did not end there.

Former Speaker of the House and a republican politician, Newt Gingrich tells Megyn Kelly
"I mean, do you want to go back through the tapes on your show recently?" he asked. "You are fascinated with sex, and you don't care about public policy."

Kelly asked if Trump was a "sexual predator" after mentioning a hot-mic "Access Hollywood" tape from 2005 in which Trump boasted of being able to grope women without their consent because he claimed to be famous. The Republican nominee described his comments as a "locker room banter." and nothing more.

Kelly said in an interview with Charlie Rose on October 8th, 2015 that neither she nor Fox News wanted "any sort of war" with Trump.

Kelly added "He was obviously upset. That's fine. He's running for president, it's not a fun business, there's going to be ups and downs, and I know he considered that a down," On the same interview she mentioned. "So we just wanted to forge forward and try to put it behind us, not pour any more fuel on that fire."

After the interview, Kelly made it clear that she wouldn't engage in a strife with Trump. However, there is no stopping Trump's agenda against Kelly. This prompted the news anchor to respond to social media after a series of attacks thrown at her.

In a series of tweet exchanges, Trump tweeted "Isn't it terrible that @megynkelly used a poll not used before (I.B.D.) when I was down but refuses to use it now when I am up?"

To which Megyn Kelly replied with a picture of result polls and a tweet saying "@realDonaldTrump - Facts matter."
Kelly was able to discuss the matter with ABC News last February.

Kelly told ABC News "It was bizarre because I became the story. He was so very focused on me that I became the story, and you know, you never want to be the story when you're a news person," she said. "You want to be covering the story, so it was like an 'Alice Through the Looking Glass' experience."

In a one-on-one interview with Trump that aired last May, Kelly, said it took her a while to find the right time to reach out to Trump.

"In April there was a lull in the tweet storm, and I seized on the opportunity," Kelly added. "I had been looking for months for just the right window to go in there. But every time I thought I was there, he'd start up again, whether it was boycotting the second Fox News debate or calling me crazy and sick after the third debate."

During Kelly's the interview with Trump, the real estate mogul said he thought Kelly's question about his comments about women "was unfair" but seemed to realize her decision to ask it. He said "I don't really blame you because you're doing your thing. But from my standpoint, I don't have to like it."

The months following the interview the tension between Trump and Kelly seemed to have eased with no significant flare-ups.

Shortly after the election Megyn Kelly left the Fox Network to go to NBC.

Max Vanguard

Chapter 3

CLINTON AND TRUMP POSITIONS

Clinton for higher Taxes vs. Trump for lower taxes

Clinton and Trump have very different points of view regarding taxes. Here is Hillary's position:

"I want to make sure the wealthy pay their fair share, which they have not been doing. I want the Buffett Rule to be in effect, where millionaires have to pay 30 percent tax rates instead of 10 percent to nothing in some cases. I want to make sure we rein in the excessive use of political power to feather the nest and support the super wealthy."

Here is Trump's position:

"Middle-income Americans and businesses will experience profound relief, and taxes will be greatly simplified for everyone. I mean everyone. Reducing taxes will cause new companies and new jobs to come roaring back into our country."

Clinton for Free Trade vs. Trump for Fair Trade

Americans have been presented with a diverse set of trade policies both nominees. On Clinton's side, she has rejected CAFTA and the TPP yet finds that the worldwide economy needs free trade. While Trump disputes for a more Protectionist financial approach in saying "Our nation is getting ripped off."

Worldwide trade is both a complicated and notable topic that Americans ought to consider when voting in the year's presidential election. Trump pushes for a more safe position on trade which is like Mercantilism. In layman terms, protectionism contends for a "great balance of trade" by sending out more than bringing in and ensuring domestic industries rivaling imported products by means of taxes. Trump said that he would renegotiate NAFTA and force a 35% tax on Mexican imports. With Chinese imports, Trump needs to require a 45% duty. In the first presidential debate between Clinton and Trump, Trump said "We have to renegotiate our trade deals. And, Lester, they're taking our jobs, they're giving incentives, they're doing things that, frankly, we don't do. Let me give you the example of Mexico. They have a VAT tax. We're on a different system. When we sell into Mexico, there's a tax. When they sell in -- automatic, 16 percent, approximately. When they sell into us, there's no tax. It's a defective agreement. It's been defective for a long time, many years, but the politicians haven't done anything about it."
Trump is showing here that laws or action of other countries can give them an advantage. Thus a tax to equalize or make the trade fair or equal for both countries needs to be put in place.

Put differently; free trade can take into consideration inventive consumption to occur. Trump said "I am all for free trade, but it's got to be fair. When Ford moves their massive plants to Mexico, we get nothing." Trump is correct because the record shows there were employment issues in the manufacturing industry and NAFTA and unfair trade or manipulated trade is to blame.

Trump is vocal about supporting free trade but is also insisted that "the problem with free trade is you need really talented people to negotiate for you." One coherence with Trump is that he supposes America is being exploited. For instance, on the TPP Trump believes China is going to "come in, as they always do, through the back door and take advantage of everyone." On global exchange arrangements like NAFTA and TPP, Clinton adopts an alternate strategy. Clinton has altered her opinion on the TPP. At first, she called it, the "gold standard" of trade. Later she said, "I absorbed new info and changed my mind to oppose TPP." This kind of fluctuating on global trade strategies is something Clinton has been scrutinized for.

Clinton for Open Borders vs Trump for Closed borders

On the third presidential debate, the candidates couldn't avoid wandering off topic and not addressing the topic as flat out as the topic deserves, however, they raised some essential points and their stance on immigration turned out to be clear.

Trump began by connecting illegal immigration to the country's the drug trade. While drugs are fundamentally a U.S. Customs and Border Protection issue, there is no denying that unlawful immigration is a component of drug trafficking. Trump mentioned, that there are criminals infiltrating the United States over the U.S.- Mexican border.

His point that whether we are a nation or not, relies on upon whether we have a border or not, is essentially right. This analysis, in a manner of speaking, is correct. Trump points out that the best solution for the issue is building a divider over the southern border and have Mexico pay for it.

Unlike Trump's wall proposition, Hillary Clinton did not give solid recommendations around this issue. She doesn't agree with Trump about building a wall, in spite of the fact that there are unlawful migrants going over the borders. She did say however that all violent criminal immigrants ought to be deported. However, it is more likely that she should just turn a blind eye to illegal immigration as President Obama has done for the eight years of his presidency.

Clinton discussed a path to citizenship for the 11 million unlawful immigrants in the US, claiming that their legalization will bring them out of the shadows and along these lines make America more secure. Clinton said she would take a shot at comprehensive immigration reform within her first 100 days of her Presidency.

Donald Trump explains that all illegal migrant should be extradited from the United States. While over the span of the campaign he has mellowed his position on this issue to some degree, despite everything he holds this view. The issue for Trump on this position is a legal due process. In the United States, we have a constitutional right to due process. This applies to anybody in the country. It implies that there must be legal oversight to deporting foreigners.

More than anything, the debate exchanges just touched the surface of the elaborate issue of migration in the United States.

Clinton for ObamaCare vs Trump for Getting rid of Obamacare

At the focal point of the debate among the presidential hopefuls is President Barack Obama's 2010 health care trademark, Obamacare. Previous President Bill Clinton, spouse of Democratic presidential nominee Hillary Clinton, called the health care law "the craziest thing on the planet" then attempting to stroll back his remarks a day later.

The former president also added "So you've got this crazy system where all of a sudden 25 million more people have health care and then the people who are out there busting it, sometimes 60 hours a week, wind up with their premiums doubled and their coverage cut in half. It's the craziest thing in the world," probing the Affordable Care Act which has produced an increasing number of premiums for middle-class Americans who don't qualify for subsidies.

As a part of her health care plan, Hillary Clinton, as per MedScape, needs to amend Obamacare by expanding on the working parts of the law and widen the insurance coverage while bringing down the expenses of exchange plan premiums and high deductibles

Clinton wants an administration-run health plan or "open choice" in each state to contend with private plans in the trades and would bring down the maximum amount that a person needs to contribute toward a premium. She would likewise make an expense credit of up to $2500 per individual or $5000 per family to counterbalance out-of-pocket spending that surpasses 5 percent of wage. The Democratic nominee would likewise bring down the age that Americans can get into Medicare to 55.

She likewise tended to some Obamacare's issues amid the second presidential debate, when she was questioned regarding the increasing expenses of medical coverage premiums. To which the secretary of state replied "I'm going to fix it because I agree with you. Premiums have gotten too high. Copays, deductibles, prescription drug costs. I've laid out a series of actions that we can take to try to get those costs down,"

The Secretary of state also added, "I don't want people to forget when we're talking about reining in the costs, which has to be the highest priority of the next president when the Affordable Care Act passed, it wasn't just that 20 million got insurance who didn't have it before. But that in and of itself was a good thing. I meet these people all the time, and they tell me what a difference having that insurance meant to them and their families."

Hillary was firm on her statement about Affordable Medical Care saying "I want very much to save what works and is good about the

Affordable Care Act. But we've got to get costs down. We've got to provide additional help to small businesses so that they can afford to provide health insurance. But if we repeal it, as Donald has proposed, and start over again, all of those benefits I just mentioned are lost to everybody, not just people who get their health insurance on the exchange. And then we would have to start all over again,"

Trump, on the other hand, has systematically vowed that if he is elected president, he will abolish Obamacare and replace it with free-market resolutions for uninsured or underinsured Americans.

Under Tump's plan, health insurers could sell policies across state lines. The New York City billionaire said this will open competition. People could also use pre-tax dollars to obtain coverage and individuals could open health savings accounts under Trump's plan. Open-ended federal contributions to state Medicaid programs with stop grants intended to give states more freedom in spending the money.

Trump's seven-point scheme highlighted on his website which promotes cutting waste and less expensive medication costs would likewise require value transparency from all medical services suppliers, particularly specialists and social insurance associations like centers and healing facilities. He contends that people ought to have the capacity to shop, to locate the best costs for exams or other medicinal related procedure.

What's more, the businessman turned politician is supporting for the dismissal of limits to passage into free markets for medication suppliers that offer reliable, safe, and less expensive products. Congress will require the guts to step far from the uncommon interests and make the right decision for America, he contends. He clarifies that in spite of the fact that the pharmaceutical business is in the private division, drug organizations provide a public service. Trump believes that permitting consumers access to import safe and dependable drugs from abroad will bring more alternatives.

The Republican bet is also an advocate of improving mental health plans. "Families, without the ability to get the information needed to help those who are ailing, are too often not given the tools to help their loved ones. There are promising reforms being developed in Congress that should receive bi-partisan support," as stated on his website. Trump also added during the second presidential debate, "Obamacare is a disaster. You know it. We all know it. It's going up at numbers that nobody's ever seen worldwide. Nobody's ever seen numbers like this for health care."

Trump claimed that it was excessively costly for people as well as for the nation.

He explained, "It's going to be one of the biggest line items very shortly. We have to repeal it and replace it with something absolutely much less expensive and something that works, where your plan can actually be tailored. We have to get rid of the lines around the state, artificial lines, where we stop insurance companies from coming in and competing because they want and President Obama and whoever was working on it, they want to leave those lines, because that gives the insurance companies essentially monopolies. We want competition!"

Other Positions

GUN CONTROL

Growing firearm control has been a political non-starter for a considerable length of time. The 1994 restriction on assault weapons lapsed in 2004. In recent years, many states have extended gun rights, and also the rundown of places where guns are permitted. Mass shootings regularly incite gun-control advocates to request that Congress grow regulations, most recently after 49 individuals were slaughtered at an Orlando, Florida club this year. However, those efforts are yet to obtain results.

Extending gun rights has been one of Donald

Trump's most constant messages. The Republican candidate calls for upholding gun laws as of and for a rigorous pursuance of violent criminals. Trump's firearm policies likewise call for extending treatment programs for those with psychological problems.

Mr. Trump resists growing the system used to check the backgrounds of gun buyers to include all the deals at gun shows. He calls bans on firearms and magazines "a total failure." On his site, he says: "Law-abiding people should be allowed to own the firearm of their choice." He additionally pushes for a national right to carry that would consider concealed carry licenses from each state. The National Rifle Association has supported Trump on his stance.

Clinton calls for comprehensive background checks that would require all weapon buyers, including all clients at firearm shows, to be cleared through the National Instant Criminal Background Check System. Current law applies to buy through government authorized merchants and does exclude deals by private people. She bolsters changing the law that permits a weapon deal to continue if the FBI has been notable within three business days to find proof to deny that deal. She criticizes the three-day constrain for permitting Dylann Roof to buy the firearm he is associated with using in the 2015 mass shooting at the Emanuel AME Church in Charleston, S.C.

Mrs. Clinton likewise says the laws ought to be adapted to keep firearms out of the hands of domestic abusers, and she is for putting a limitation on what she describes as military-style weapons. She has been supported by a variety of gun-control promotion groups, including the Brady Campaign to Prevent Gun Violence.

GAY AND TRANSGENDER RIGHTS

Trump and Clinton lie on different pages of many gay and transgender rights issues. Clinton is for marriage rights for same-sex couples, Trump, on the other hand, contradicts this position. She argues a North Carolina law, seen by transgender individuals and others as biased that require everybody to use the public restroom equal to the sex recorded on their birth certificate. Mr. Trump approves the existing law. Be that as it may, while Clinton has attempted to highlight her perspectives on gay and transgender rights, Trump hardly says his.

Trump contradicts the Supreme Court choice allowing a national right to same-sex marriage. However, Trump doesn't display his worries about same-sex marriage with the same intensity and passion as that of its adversaries. Asked on Fox News in January if he would select judges to overrule the court decision, he replied, "I would strongly consider that, yes." After a terror attack at a gay night club in Florida, Trump took on the role as a protector of gay and transgender rights, saying he would keep conceivably dangerous Muslim immigrants out of the US.

At first, the business mogul said he was against the North Carolina law on open bathrooms and said that Caitlyn Jenner, a reality star transgender, would be welcome to choose any lavatory of her choice at Trump Tower. Mr. Trump later said he upheld the state's choice to pass the law.

The former first lady turned secretary of state Clinton restricted gay marriage until 2013, favoring common unions. She said her perspectives grew. Before changing her position on same-sex marriage, Clinton had bolstered equal rights on different matters. As secretary of state, she conveyed a speech in 2011 proclaiming that "gay rights are human rights."

Clinton supported the Obama government on its direction in allowing public school students to utilize the bathroom depending on their personal sexual orientation. She supports legislation banning discrimination on the premise of sexual orientation or gender identity in business, housing, public accommodations and different regions. The video declaring her nomination included a gay couple, and her presidential battle has effectively sought gay and lesbian voters.

GENERAL ELECTIONS

Chapter 4

WIKILEAKS

WikiLeaks has released thousands of emails that were hacked from Hillary Clinton's campaign chairman John Podesta as well as other sources.

The first revelation that the WikiLeaks brought to light was that Hillary Clinton has a very close and cozy relationship with the United States main stream media. Donna Brazile, a high level Democate, working for CNN gave Mrs. Clinton's campaign question for upcoming presidential debates.

The WikiLeaks cesspool of John Podesta's emails has uncovered the corruption and deference of Clinton's battle campaign and even her time in office. Issues and revelations came on a daily basis and to such extent that her team had difficulty in keeping track of each one. So here are the top 10 misleading, deceitful discoveries uncovered thus far.

1. Mrs. Clinton had sheltered and odd relationship with the people in media.

> Donna Brazile, a CNN contributor and then consultant to the Democratic Nation Committee gave the Clinton campaign team advanced copy of the CNN town lobby question that she thought would give Clinton some time.

Mrs. Clinton's campaign praised a New York Times columnist for "teeing up" stories for them, and ABC's George Stephanopoulos for pounding home their ideas. The Boston Globe helped Mrs. Clinton's group augment her essence in New England amid the primaries and CNBC's John Harwood gloated to them about hounding Donald Trump during a Republican debate he moderated.

2. The State Department paid special regard on the "Friends of Bill."

After the massive 2010 Haiti earthquake, a senior aide to then-Secretary of State Clinton repeatedly gave special attention to those identified by the abbreviations "FOB" (Friends of Bill) or "WJC VIPs" (William Jefferson Clinton VIPs), referring to the former president. The emails show Mrs. Clinton's State Department prioritized and benefited Mr. Clinton's friends in the $10 billion recovery effort. The State Department also polled the popularity of Mr. Clinton in Haiti and shared the results with him.

3. Mrs. Clinton fought for "a hemispheric common market with open trade and open borders."

Mrs. Clinton's vision for America to be like the European Union. She reportedly informed investors in a paid speech last 2013 to Brazilian Banco Itau: "My dream is a hemispheric common market, with open trade and open borders, sometime in the future with energy that's as green and sustainable as we can get it, powering growth and opportunity for every person in the hemisphere." Without borders, there are no countries, including the United States.

4. The Clinton campaign was talking with the Department of Justice officials regarding the release of her emails.

Brian Fallon, Mrs. Clinton's representative, and previous Justice Department staff member seemed to have conversations with sources inside the DOJ about progressing open records claims to ask for access to her messages while filling in as secretary of state. In an email from May 2015, Mr. Fallon said that "DOJ folks" had "informed" him about the up and coming status meeting in one of the claim.

5. The Clinton camp was given information on the release of the Benghazi emails.

In April 2015, Clinton crusade Deputy Communications Director Kristina Schake alluded to a "tip" from a source with respect to when the State Department intended to discharge Mrs. Clinton's Benghazi messages. Mrs. Clinton's legal counselor Heather Samuelson followed up on the tip, expressing: "Latest: Still aiming for Friday, but potential it gets delayed until early next week because still moving through interagency review process. Will check back tomorrow and keep you posted. Quick update on this — DOS says the release of the 300 will likely happen on Thurs or Friday. Will keep you posted as I hear anything further on my end. Thx."

6. Mrs. Clinton admitted that sometimes her public and private positions vary.

In a speech made in 2013 in front of the National Multi-Housing Council, Mrs. Clinton pointed out that her public positions may vary with her private positions, since legislative issues is a monstrous business.

Politics is like sausage being made," Mrs. Clinton said. "It is unsavory, and it always has been that way, but we usually end up where we need to be. But if everybody's watching, you know, all of the backroom discussions and the deals, you know, then people get a little nervous, to say the least. So, you need both a public and a private position."

.

7. Mrs. Clinton's representative taunted Catholics and evangelicals as "severely backwards."

Hacked emails demonstrate Mrs. Clinton's campaign representative Jennifer Palmieri and other Clinton associates straightforwardly discussing Catholics being "severely backwards" and imposing that they don't understand "what the hell they're talking about." The April 2011 dialog between Ms. Palmieri and John Halpin, of the liberal Center for American Progress, taunts media magnate Rupert Murdoch for bringing his kids up in the Catholic Church and said that most "powerful elements" in the conservative movement are Catholics.

8. Mrs. Clinton acknowledged she experienced difficulties relating to the battles of the middle class.

In a 2014 speech for Goldman Sachs and BlackRock, Mrs. Clinton revealed her wealth and open persona way of life segregated her from the money related struggles of the vast majority of the nation, saying her recollections of her youth is the way she associates now to regular Americans. "Obviously, I'm kind of far removed because the life I've lived and the economic, you know, fortunes that my husband and I now enjoy," Mrs. Clinton said of identifying with the working class.

9. Mrs. Clinton campaign utilized Benghazi as a diversion from the email scandal.

Mrs. Clinton's campaign attempted to make her email scandal fade amid the Benghazi inquiry by attempting to conflate and confound the two separate occurrences. Mr. Podesta advised assistants in March 2015 to direct the media's concentration from the email outrage to the House Benghazi examination, which they felt had just been painted in the media as a Republican witch chase.

10. The Clinton group strategized on the best way to postpone discharging emails, knowing it was illegal.

In the wake of accepting a subpoena for her emails, Clinton insider Phillipe Reines in March 2015 talked about tactics to use as a reason not to discharge every last bit of her email. It seemed to constitute a cognizant effort of the Clinton camp to baffle and defer a congressional subpoena. Mr. Reines said of the emails: "Not flippantly, and maybe just from

Nick's [Merrill, Clinton spokesman] mouth —
but rather than going around on how to release
the 55k let's just be for what's happening and
use this as an excuse. Because we can say even
if State has equities, not providing them would
put her in legal jeopardy OR we can say happy
for them to have it, happy for them to have
them as soon as State is comfortable."

TRUMP'S $900 MILLION LOSS

Donald Trump's federal tax returns from 1995, were illegally disclosed by the media. Trump's taxes reportedly showing that he held a $916 million loss, as published by the New York Times, which said it obtained three pages of Trump's tax history documents that year. The documents supposedly came in by mail with a New York City postmark on.

Apparently, the loss was from three of Trump's asset which is his New York, New Jersey and Connecticut state tax filings that were dated way back in 1995. The document showed a $915,729,293 in total losses.

The New York Times paper said the authenticity of the documents was verified by Jack Mitnick, a lawyer and certified public accountant who managed Trump's tax obligations until 1996 and who was believed to be Trump's tax adviser as prepared in one of Trump's New Jersey tax form.

Trump's camp replied to the Times story by issuing a statement that did not affirm or deny the legality of the documents that the New York Times posted, saying "The only news here is that the more than 20-year-old alleged tax document was illegally obtained." The statement also writes, "Mr. Trump has paid hundreds of millions of dollars in property taxes, sales and excise taxes, real estate taxes, city taxes, state taxes, employee taxes and federal taxes."

TRUMP TAPE WITH BILLY BUSH

Bush in a statement said he was "embarrassed and ashamed." However, Trump consistently denied having groped women.

Bush, who had remained at "Today" for two months, is the nephew of Republican former President George H.W. Bush.

Bush, a father of three, said in the note declaring his leaving and that he was "deeply grateful for the conversations I've had with my daughters, and for all of the support from family, friends, and colleagues. I look forward to what lies ahead."

In the 2005 recording, which was first reported by The Washington Post, Trump discusses fruitlessly seeking a relationship with another "Access Hollywood" employee, Nancy O'Dell.

In the 2005 tape, which was initially uncovered by The Washington Post, Trump talks about unsuccessfully looking for an affair with a certain Nancy O'Dell an "Access Hollywood" employee.

We've pulled some of the lines from Trump from the tape saying "I moved on her and I failed. I'll admit it. I did try and f*** her. She was married," he also mentioned "I've gotta use some Tic Tacs, just in case I start kissing her. You know I'm automatically attracted to beautiful" The then newly married Trump added "I just start kissing them. It's like a magnet. Just kiss. I don't even wait."

However one of the most disturbing and what stuck to most people was Trump saying "And when you're a star, they let you do it. You can do anything. Grab them by the p*ssy, you can do anything."

The two men talked about an actress who was waiting at the end of their bus ride. When they got off, Bush pushed the woman to hug Trump and said, "how about a little hug for the Bushy?"

After the issue on the tape recording got out of hand NBC was quick to decide in firing "Today" show host Billy Bush. The network has initially issued a suspension two days after the tape was reported on October 8.

NBC issued a statement saying "Billy Bush will be leaving the TODAY show's 9 a.m. hour, effective today." The note also said "While he was a new member of the TODAY team, he was a valued colleague and longtime member of the broader NBC family. We wish him success as he goes forward."

Billy Bush's lawyers had since been arranging terms of his exit before the announcement. The settlement with NBC did exclude a non-contend statement, which means Bush "is a free agent," his legal advisor, Marshall Grossman told the Associated Press. Financial terms of the arrangement were kept classified.

During the second presidential deliberation, Trump said that he never did any of the activities heard on the tape, saying "this was locker room banter, a private conversation that took place many years ago. Bill Clinton has said far worse to me on the golf course — not even close. I apologize if anyone was offended."

Melania, Trump's new wife was quick to help out her husband on the issue, and during a CNN interview she said "I wonder if they even knew the mic was on," Melania added that it was just "boy talk, and he was led on — like egged on — from the host to say dirty and bad stuff."

Regardless of Trump's statement, different women have since accused the business tycoon and said that they had an encounter with him in the past by grabbing or peculiarly kissing them on the lips. However after Trump was elected president all these accusers decided to take no action. Many of the accusers were also found to be lying. Did Hillary pay these women to come forward? Why did not one of them take any kind of action against Trump with the first 100 days of Trump being elected.

REPUBLICANS NOT SUPPORTING TRUMP

The Republican Party conveyed a remarkable and a surprising ignore to their particular presidential candidate Donald Trump as the Bush family and Speaker of the House of Representatives Paul Ryan, declined to support him.

Paul Ryan, the 54th and current Speaker of the House of Representatives, said he was "not ready" to support Mr Trump, also stating that the time had come to "set aside bullying and belittlement".

This was during Trump's attempt to find a vice-presidential running mate, finding himself rejected after his three initial choices.

Adding up to the list is 2012 Republican Presidential nominee, Mitt Romney. Romney declared that he would not attend the party's scheduled July convention.

The developments pointed the degree of the division and spite immersing the Republicans, and the overwhelming errand Mr. Trump faces to bring together the party.

Hillary Clinton, which at that time stands as a plausible Democratic nominee, tried to underwrite by releasing TV commercial which demonstrated Trump being denounced by fellow Republicans.

The advertisement featured Jeb Bush stating that Mr. Trump "needs therapy" and Marco Rubio referring to him as "the most vulgar person ever to aspire to the presidency."

Trump tried to get back at Jeb Bush during the nomination process suggesting that Jeb has "low energy" and is considered to be an "embarrassment to his family". Jeb Bush's father, former President George H W Bush, had eagerly supported the Republican nominee in each of the five races since he went out, however, his representative said he would not do as such this time. Also, Freddy Ford, a representative for previous President George W Bush, said he "does not plan to participate in or comment on the presidential campaign".

The Rolling Stones also pressed in against Mr. Trump, trying to prevent him from using their music at political assemblies. The British rock band, of which Mr. Trump is a fan, said they had "requested that he cease all use immediately".

Colin Powell, the 65th United States Secretary of State reportedly told the Long Island Association that he is rooting for the Presidential Democratic Party nominee Hillary Clinton.

In spite of the fact that he Powell is considered to be a long-standing Republican, his choice to embrace a Democrat is not surprising. He likewise sponsored Barack Obama in both 2008 and 2012.

Nor is it shocking that he would contradict Trump. A comprehensive number of officers, particularly those in the anti-extremist establishment, have reprimanded Trump as favorable to Russia, a nation which is considered to be partially sensitive to the significance of America's key partners, in addition to many other things.

POLLS SHOWING A LESS POPULAR CLINTON AND TRUMP

Donald Trump and Hillary Clinton are considered to be the two most unpopular presidential candidates in more than 30 years of surveys and polling; this is according to ABC News/Washington polls. Studies show that among U.S. adult voters, Clinton has a 59% negative rating, statistically tied with Trump who has a 60% negative rating.

In another survey done by ABC News/Washington Post, 57 percent said they had an adverse feeling of Clinton and Trump. The remaining 46 percent stated they do not have an amicable feeling for Clinton's candidacy and 45 percent have the same to say about Trump.

Of course, we've never had two candidates like this, about whom so many voters had already made up their minds — undoubtedly. It'll be fascinating to perceive how it plays out. Voters see this campaign, as a decision between the lesser of two shades of evils.

Many Americans who detest Clinton say she is not credible. This remained to be one of the eminent concerns behind her candidacy. One-third of Americans claimed she is corrupt. On top of that, the remaining third half said her positions change depending on which the wind blows, which appears a culmination of her integrity. Following these bases, some of her critics even accused the secretary of state as an "unfit" candidate for the presidency and added that she doesn't know enough about the issues.

Trump, on the other hand, faces a different set of challenges among voters.

While Trump, an extremely rich New Yorker, doesn't need to dig the ground to hurt Clinton's candidacy, his issues are also very visible. A fourth of his adversaries said racism is his greatest imperfection. Considering that there are Hispanic and Black-American voters that live in the United States. The percentage of people who would not vote for him reflected a huge 40 percent of Black voters and 35 percent of the Hispanic voters. Another 20 percent claimed that Trump does not have the right experience and background for politics more so the presidency.

This campaign is a battle and a choice between the lesser two evils. Although, it is obviously during the surveys that a variety of voters had undoubtedly decided. The battle remained to be an entertaining and interesting show to watch.

TRUMP'S CARD AGAINST BILL CLINTON

It was clear that Donald Trump was on the defensive, following the two days of conflict and rejection of Trump by many Republicans over a 2005 tape of him and Billy Bush talking about how women in very poor light.

Only an hour and a half before the second Presidential Debate between Trump and Clinton, the businessman turned politician held a surprise live broadcast on Facebook with the ladies who have accused Bill Clinton of sexual assault and in some cases the women accused Hillary of covering it up and turning a blind eye to what had happened.

The women include Juanita Broaddrick, Paula Jones, Kathleen Willey and Kathy Shelton. After Trump addresses his comments on the leaked tape he introduced the ladies and said: "These four very courageous women have asked to be here, and it was our honor to help them."

One of the accusers, Broaddrick previously signed an affidavit stating that Bill Clinton did not rape her, but later retracted her affidavit. Broaddrick said "Actions speak louder than words," she went on and added "Mr. Trump may have said some bad words, but Bill Clinton raped me and Hillary Clinton threatened me. I don't think there's anything worse."

Max Vanguard

The surprise forum and the frill of the particular subject are remarkable on the eve of a debate, primarily for a presidential campaign.

TRUMP'S ACCUSERS

During the second presidential debate, the then debate host and CNN news anchor Anderson Cooper professed a question directed toward the Republican nominee Donald Trump on the released 2005 Access Hollywood video that found him saying that he felt entitled to "grab them by the pussy." "For the record, you're stating you never did that?" the news anchor pushed. Trump, making light of his comments as "locker room talk," denied he had ever kissed or grabbed ladies without permission. "No one has more respect for women than I do." Trump added.

His dissent, however, has invited women who are currently accusing him to press charges and complaints. These women blame the real estate mogul for indecent behavior from grabbing on planes to undesirable approaches in the Trump Tower.

The presidential hopeful has firmly denied the attribution. His campaign team in a desperate move and warn lawsuits against those media outlets who distributed unverified claims.

First, a secret recording captured Donald Trump that he groped and kissed women without their consent. At that point, came reports that on The Howard Stern Show in 2005, Trump himself told the host that he walked into dressing rooms while pageant contestants were exposed. Presently more than twelve ladies have approached, both distinctly and secretly, to attest to the fact that Trump did precisely that.

Some of Trump's accusers were driven to speak out after hearing Trump's statement that he had not grabbed women without their permission. Motivated by the recording between Trump and Bush, concerning Trump gloating about grabbing and kissing women.

Listed below are some of the names of the accusers and their brief encounter with Trump.

Ivana Trump, Trump's ex-wife
In spite of the fact that she now says her story was "without legitimacy," in a separation statement in 1992, Ivana Trump depicted a vicious sexual assault by her then-husband.

Kristin Anderson, former model
Trump came to up her skirt at a dance club without having been introduced to her and touched her vagina through her clothing, she said.

Temple Taggart, Pageant contestant - Miss Utah 1997
The shocked 21-year-old Miss Utah title holder was shocked when the business mogul introduced

himself by kissing her on the lips.

Mariah Billado, Pageant contestant - Miss Vermont Teen USA 1997
Billado claimed that while they were naked and about to change Trump suddenly barged into their dressing room. Billado and a few other contestants ages 15 to 19 were present during this incident.
Karena Virginia, Yoga instructor
Virginia alleged Trump of grabbing her by the arm and touching her breast back in 1998 US open when she was waiting for a car service outside the venue.

Tasha Dixon, Pageant contestant - Miss Arizona 2001
Dixon has the same claims with Mariah Billado. Dixon who was 18 at the time of the 2001 pageant, stated that Trump "just came strolling right on in," when the contestants were changing into bikinis.

Natasha Stoynoff, former People magazine reporter.
Stoynoff was assigned to cover Trump during the early 2000s. Stoynoff claimed that during the time that she was working on a news feature on Trump. The businessman pushed her against the wall and sexually assaulted her and said: "We're going to have an affair."

Jessica Leeds, Businesswoman

She had a chance to sit with Trump during a flight, who she claimed grabbed her breasts and tried to reach up her skirt.

Lisa Boyne, Health food entrepreneur
At a dinner, Trump looked up women's skirts and commented on their underwear and genitalia.

Jill Harth, makeup artist
Harth got the chance to met with Trump during a business deal and alleged Trump of repeatedly kissing and groping her.

Summer Zervos, The Apprentice contestant
Zervos claimed that when she visited Trump in his New York office, the real estate mogul kissed her on the lips. Invited her for supper, but rather took her to a hotel, grabbed her and attempted to engage in sexual relations with her.

Some of these women have had stories that have not checked out, while others claimed they have told people at the time when the alleged event occurred. But none have brought forward any direct proof that any of these events occurred. However, that does not mean that the alleged incident did not occur, it just means that by law a person is deemed innocent until proven guilty in front of a court.

Did these women came forward wanting to ride the publicity of the Trump and Bush tape? Were they offered some kind of financial support by the

Clinton Campaign, or were they just trying to help the Hillary campaign.

The fact is we don't know why these women came forward, but we do know that based on the information that we have gathered from other witnesses, they are stating that most of Trump's accusers are not telling the truth about the incident.

A strong testament to this is, not one of these women has brought any legal case against Trump. Even after the first 100 days of his presidency.

Max Vanguard

TRUMP AND CLINTON PERCEPTION BY PEOPLE

From the begin of the campaign period, people were skeptical on who to choose between Clinton or Trump because people believe that it will be a battle between two leaders neither of which they want to be president.

On a survey done using registered voters as correspondents, only 27% of them said that Trump would make a good president. 15% say he would be an average.

Perspectives of a potential Hillary Clinton administration are just to some degree less negative. Around three-in-ten (31%) say she would be an awesome or great president, contrasted and 22% who say she would be normal and 12% who think she would make a poor president. While 33% of the correspondents say Clinton would be terrible as a president.

Supporters of Trump and Clinton are confident that their bet would perform an excellent job as a president. A 68%-in general of Trump supporters says that he would make a great (23%) or good (45%) president. This is very similar what Clinton got in terms of positive views.

Of course both Democrats and Republicans are

included in these polls. So what we can conclude is that both candidates are either loved or hated by people based on these limited polls.

Clinton not telling the truth

People do not want to trust Hillary Clinton because of the email server scandal, Wikileaks because Clinton has stated that she had multiple positions on the issues because of her past. However, most people that don't trust her can describe her in one word, "liar."

According to a Washington Post-ABC News poll done in March 2016, 37% of Americans said that they trust Clinton. Three months later, another survey done by Rasmussen found that 46% of the people surveyed said that Clinton was less honest compared to other politicians

This couldn't be more suitable to a government official like Clinton, who is infamous because of her private email server controversies not to mention being caught numerous times for delivering misleading statements and telling half truths and lies. And now more than ever, with left and right evidence, Hillary Clinton's political career has been painted by deceit.

Hillary Lied about Classified information being sent to her private unsanctioned email server. James Comey the director of the FBI testified that there was classified email sent to Hillary's server at a congressional hearing.   Comey called Hillary "extremely careless"

"I'm not making excuses," Clinton said at a rally in Ohio. "I've said it was a mistake and I regret it," said Clinton in one of her rallies.

Clinton insisted that "what I did was allowed." She maintained that she "opted for convenience to use my personal email account, which was allowed by the State Department, because I thought it would be easier to carry just one device for my work and for my personal emails instead of two." However these statements are not true. The government does not allow classified material to be stored on unsecure systems. Hillary's system was unsecure.

A political consultant insisted that the more Clinton "can do to change the subject so her conversations are around the topics" and matters her campaign is concerned with, the better. This is apparently the best move that the Democratic nominee can do to shift attention away from all the controversies surrounding her.

Trump calling women degrading names

Republican presidential candidate Donald Trump says he can't particularly remember offending women, however, there are always two sides of a story. According to some of Trump's accusers Trump had a history of mainly relating women to animals.

Here are some of the instances on which Donald Trump has allegedly displayed lack of class and has shamed women.

Back in 2012, the business mogul aimed at the co-founder and editor-in-chief of the Huffington Post, Arianna Huffington, mocking her divorce and teasing her appearance. Trump tweeted "is unattractive both inside and out. I fully understand why her former husband left her for a man—he made a good decision," referring to Huffington. Again in 2015 Trump issued a tweet saying "How much money is the extremely unattractive (both inside and out) Arianna Huffington paying her poor ex-hubby for the use of his name?"

On Celebrity Apprentice: All-Stars which aired last 2013, he fantasized on the picture of former Playboy Playmate Brande Roderick stating "It must be a pretty picture. You dropping to your knee."

He called opposing counsel in a deposition

"disgusting" for wanting to break to pump milk for her 3-month-old daughter.

In 2011 Trump attended court to testify when the complainant's lawyer Elizabeth Beck requested for a recess to breastfeed her three-month-old baby. Trump's council objected, Beck then pulled out her breast pump in hopes of proving her appeal. Trump later walked out the court room calling the Beck "disgusting".

His daughter Ivanka, is not an exception on this list. In an interview back in 2006, he joked on national television that if it weren't for a fact that Ivanka was his daughter, he would be dating her. Before that, in a 2004 radio interview, Trump told Howard Stern that he didn't mind if the host refer to Ivanka as "a piece of a**"

Also in the year 2006, Trump was caught in a quarrel with Rosie O'Donnell. The fight grew and countless shots were fired from both camp. Trump in an interview said "Rosie O'Donnell is disgusting, both inside and out. If you take a look at her, she's a slob. How does she even get on television? If I were running The View, I'd fire Rosie. I'd look her right in that fat, ugly face of hers and say, 'Rosie, you're fired!" He added "We're all a little chubby but Rosie's just worse than most of us. But it's not the chubbiness - Rosie is a very unattractive person, both inside and out."

In Trump's book, How to Get Rich, the business tycoon wrote: "All of the women on The Apprentice flirted with me—consciously or unconsciously. That's to be expected."

Even the biggest of all celebrities is on the list. When Angelina Jolie had a falling out with her father Jon Voight, Trump was ask to give a statement on CNN's Larry King. Trump went on saying "I really understand beauty. And I will tell you, she's not - I do own Miss Universe. I do own Miss USA. I mean I own a lot of different things. I do understand beauty, and she's not."

Trump has lost the support of leading Republicans. A number of Republicans has already called that the 70-year-old businessman drops out from the race.

Trump refuse to drop out of the race and issued a statement apologizing for his conduct. Later when pressed by multiple people to drop out of the presidential race and let Hillary win, Trump indicated that he would get back on track issuing a statement saying "I'd never withdraw. I've never withdrawn in my life. No, I'm not quitting this race. I have tremendous support."

TRUMP RALLIES VS CLINTON RALLIES

During the 2016 presidential campaign, we saw Republican nominee Donald Trump gather a huge crowd on his speeches in convention centers, parks, and even airport hangars. However, Hillary Clinton's rallies were small and even at times with only a few hundred people. Sources said that she and her campaign team apparently struggled to be able to fill small colleges and community centers. The news media would not cover this, and almost never showed the empty halls where Hillary campaigned.

It seemed as if the only way Clinton was able to get any kind of crowd would be when she brought in some other star to help her out. Political names like First Lady Michelle Obama, Senator Bernie Sanders and even the President himself Barack Obama were there to show their support. Towards the end of the campaign, the former first lady even invited big celebrity names like Jay-Z, Pharrell Williams, and Katy Perry. It was evident that Clinton's campaign team did the best they could but fell short in making a significant impact at Clinton's rallies.

In Tempe, Arizona, a place that is not a popular campaign stop compared to Florida, Wisconsin, New Hampshire and Pennsylvania; Clinton was able to pack more than 10,000 people in attendance. A political analyst explained that this was expected in Arizona as the people from this state are not hounded by campaign rallies.

Trump was quick to notice the difference between his rally and Clinton's. He bragged "I have to say, we have rallies like this and we have seven, eight, nine, ten thousand routinely," in the North Carolina rally. He also added "Hillary goes out for rallies and yesterday I think she had 200 people, maybe 300."

Lara Brown, a George Washington University professor of political management, tells us that size does not always equal substance. She explains that "Trump has also regularly been going to places where he is most beloved, not where the ground game is most competitive." She also added that "Trump is a novelty and for some, to say that they went, is like saying they went to a sporting event."   Lara Brown was previously aligned with the Democrats, but later said she was more of a moderate.   Perhaps a moderate Democrat. In any case, the analysis of the ground game turned out to be wrong. Trump understood the electoral college and was able to win the election.

It is a fact that Trump held quite many more rallies than Democratic nominee Clinton. To be exact, Trump's hard work yielded him 53 more events compared to the Clinton camp. Also, math tells us that on an average Trump gets more than 6,000 people on his rallies versus Clinton who only averages about less than 1,000. That is a significant difference that may have allowed Trump to carry more of the swing states.

CLINTON 9/11 COLLAPSE

Hillary Clinton collapses, either passed out or lost control of her body, this is evident in a video clip, as she prematurely leaves from the 2016 9/11 celebration. Clinton's specialist said the scene was an aftereffect of heat and dehydration.

Clinton was seen being aided by her security detail after she fell as she was making her way to her vehicle. A news channel caught up with some witnesses and one, in particular, describes the Democratic nominee as "clearly having some type of medical episode."

Sources that spoke off the record stated that Clinton might have seizures when exposed to the sun. Other sources have indicated that Hillary has Parkinson's disease.

After over an hour of news blackout, Clinton's team released a report saying that the former First Lady "felt overheated," two days later they issued a formal statement blaming pneumonia and lack of hydration as the primary reason for the collapse

Prior the incident, Clinton was believed to have a chronic case of allergies that resulted in her having coughing fits. Clinton's physician, Dr. Lisa Bardack said in the statement. "On Friday, during follow-up evaluation of her prolonged cough, she was diagnosed with pneumonia. She was put on antibiotics and advised to rest and modify her schedule. While at this morning's event, she became overheated and dehydrated. I have just examined her and she is now re-hydrated and recovering nicely."

People accused Clinton of being awfully quiet about her health condition. This lead to the Democratic nominee's decision to release her medical records supporting her claim of good health.

Following the Clinton medical records issue, Trump also asserted on releasing his health records. A confident Trump said, "Last week I took a physical and when the numbers come in I'll be releasing very, very specific numbers." And when the businessman was asked about Clinton's health, he has this to say' "I think it's an issue."

BIAS MEDIA

When WikiLeaks released thousands of email, the cozy and inappropriate relationship between the main stream media and Hillary Clinton was exposed. John Podesta, Clinton's campaign chairman, had his email hacked. Thousands of these emails were released to the public by WikiLeaks. These emails shed light as to why the members of the press and the Democratic party nominee share a comfortable relationship.

Apparently, there were email exchanges to and from Clinton's campaign chairman John Podesta. Among the shocking revelations contained in the exchanges includes an advance copy of debate questions and the guarantee of positive coverage in favor of the Democratic nominee: Hillary Clinton.

The Democratic campaign team officials have not disavowed the validity of the emails, but rather have tried to point the finger at Russia for providing the hacked correspondence to the WikiLeaks group, and have cautioned that they could be doctored. However, to date, no series challenge with any kind of evidence concerning the validity of any of the WikiLeaks emails has occurred. Even after the first 100 days of Trump being president, there has been no evidence that the Russian's were the ones that hacked the email account of John Podesta. It could have someone from within the democratic party, or it could have been a high school hacker that guessed that the password for John Podesta's Gmail account which was 'password'.   It is laughable that someone would have a password which is 'password'. This is something a kid who watches Big Bird on Sesame Street could hack. It would not take a minor super power like Russia to hack this account. The report that this is Russia could very well be fake news put out by the main stream media as just another way to support Hillary and the Democrat party.   The Media has a real credibility issue here and there is no evidence that has been put forward that shows the Russians are to blame.

Donna Brazile, a former CNN contributor and Democratic party insider that has been the acting leader of the Democratic National Committee, messaged members of the Clinton campaign when she worked at CNN to tip them off about a question that would be asked at Clinton Bernie Sanders' debate, her strongest opponent for the Democratic primary.

Brazile sent advance notice to the Clinton camp with detail about a question concerning lead poisoning which was a question that was asked in a debate on March 6th, 2016. Later on Marth 12th Brazile passed on another question concerning the death penalty. Brazile initial denied that she gave any questions, but later came clean and admitted that she had given questions to the Clinton camp.

In another hacked email released by WikiLeaks, a staff member at The Boston Globe had all the earmarks of being contriving with Clinton's crusade to boost her so-called "presence" amid her primary race against Sanders. In the email from Marjorie Pritchard, the Globe's opinion piece supervisor, Podesta inquired as to whether the Clinton campaign was still set to present a commentary. Pritchard went ahead to offer direction on how the campaign could get an advantage by synchronizing with the Globe's standard reporting. Pritchard wrote in the email "It would be good to get it in on Tuesday, when she is in New Hampshire." And the latter part read "That would give her a big presence on Tuesday with the piece and on Wednesday with the news story. Please let me know."

Christina Reynolds, Clinton's assistant, was congratulated in a 2008 email for "single-handedly" persuading a Washington Post columnist to push a story about Cindy McCain, Arizona Sen John McCain's better half. "This is truly outstanding! Great work!" as noted by Paul Begala from the Democratic party.

The Trump campaign team issued a statement saying "We feel disappointed," Conway said. "It is disappointing to read those emails." Also, pointing out that the disclosures of secret communications between individuals from the press and the Clinton team threaten the probability of free and fair elections.   The press in the United States is given special protection, however when those protections are abused, and media try to help one political party secretly while trying to pretend that they are neutral is very dangerous. Such practices, should they continue, could lead to the media being highly regulated, and monitored by the government. This is exactly what a free nation does not want.

FBI PROBE INTO CLINTON FOUNDATION

After having been sworn as the Secretary of State During Obama's first term as President, Clinton gave her word and signed a document with the Obama administration to distance herself from the Clinton Foundation. In the agreement, Hillary agreed, that the foundation would limit incoming foreign aid and donations.

Without a doubt, several of the foundation's top donors were Foreign governments or foreign officials. The Obama administration was concern about conflict of interest between Hillary's position as Secretary of State and Hillary's role with the Clinton Foundation. However, the Obama administration could not have been that concerned since they did nothing to stop her activities.

There is an array of evidence to confirm that both Clinton and the foundation neglected to keep their word. The emails that were discovered by the FBI suggested that Clinton held her position in the foundation while holding office as the Secretary of State. The FBI had gathered proof that Clinton had allowed access and favored donors in exchange for aids to the Clinton Foundation.

Basically what happened was the following. Somebody wanted or needed the Federal government to do something, Hillary would send

Bill Clinton to give a speech for $500,000 that would be put into the foundation. Then magically what the foreign official or person needed would get done by the State Department which Hillary headed. This, of course, would be illegal for anyone to do, because it would mean that one was using their government position to enrich themselves.

Apparently, the Clinton Foundation received millions of donations from foreign governments while Hillary was Secretary of State department.

The story got its limelight because of a book was written by Peter Schweizer entitled "Clinton Cash" that allegedly uncovers pressing issues of the State Department involving big favors given to top donors of the Clinton Foundation.

An FBI investigation revealed that more than half of Clinton's private visitors during her term as the Secretary of State were donors of the Clinton Foundation. They also discovered a number of emails that suggest that donors received special access and consideration from Clinton and her office.

COLLUSION BETWEEN WHITE HOUSE, JUSTICE DEPT, MEDIA AND CLINTON CAMPAIGN

Democratic officials of the Clinton Campaign had ongoing discussions with officials within the justice department.   A WikiLeaks email from Clinton Campaign spokesman Brian Fallon said "DOJ folks" had informed him about a court hearing regarding Hillary's private email server. Republicans said that this shows a collusion between the DOJ and the Clinton Campaign. Emails retrieved through the freedom of information act show that the Obama white house was colluding with the Hillary Campaign in March of 2015. In one email from the white house communication director to the State Department. A request to cancel media appearances of John Kerry, the new secretary of state so that any questions about scandals could be avoided. In another email conversation, the state department told Hilary Clinton's legal team that they did not reveal Hilary's use of a private email server to the Congress.

The Republican National Committee additionally summoned the questionable airplane tarmac meeting between Attorney General Loretta Lynch and Bill Clinton. This meeting took place while a criminal investigation of Hillary Clinton was also taking place. It is entirely inappropriate for the Attorney General to meet with the husband of the person that is being investigated for criminal activity.

Reince Priebus, who was acting as the RNC Chairman, in a statement, said "Emails showing the Department of Justice was giving Hillary Clinton's campaign inside information about an ongoing investigation into her email server is deeply disturbing and raises, even more, questions about Bill Clinton's tarmac meeting with Attorney General Loretta Lynch."

ELECTIONS OUTCOME

Chapter 5

ELECTION EXPECTATIONS

The United States election is the electoral college system where each state that is won by a candidate provides them with a certain number of delegates. To win the presidency, a candidate must collect 270 delegates. A week before the election the survey appears there are still just enough swing states to allow for a Republican to win the presidency.

For the Republicans to win they needed to dominate in states like Pennsylvania, Michigan or Virginia, where most polling data showed the Democratic nominee leading.

Many thought it was impossible, but to some political analysts, this scenario was conceivable, and it could be supported by polling that underestimates white voter turnout or overestimates Mrs. Clinton's support in key voting demographics like blacks and the young.

For this plan to work, Trump should basically be impeccable or polling would need to be off in a mixture of distinct states that have clearly diverse voters. A mistake in New Hampshire surveying, for example, wouldn't mean calculations in Florida would probably be wrong. A miss in Michigan would have a small bearing on the outcome of Colorado.

Polls recommend that if European countries were to choose Hillary Clinton, she would unanimously win. Governments across the region are giving careful consideration and evaluating how they will function with the succeeding administration, especially if it will be led by Donald Trump.

The New York businessman-politician has discovered a few allies among a huge portion of Europe's community, both in transient vigilant Eastern Europe and in Western Europe, where against immigrant, anti- EU supporters in Germany, France, and Britain are trusting a Republican triumph will support their causes.

Trump's opinion on the sensitive subjects of migration and job are being shared by only a few people in the European nation, but, it charms him to devotees of grassroots movements over the region who see their countries as losing their authority and their business under what some see as a European super state.

According to the European foundation, their concern is about the new American leadership's ability to stay connected with Europe, therefore they are putting their bet in favor for Clinton.

German Chancellor Angela Merkel has this to say about Clinton "I admire her strategic thinking and her strong commitment to the trans-Atlantic partnership."

The Chancellor's sentiment matches that of numerous Europeans who consider Clinton to be sharing needs that are trademarks of European traditional liberalism.

A day before the election, Clinton has managed to maintain her edge in the polls. In a race between a Democrat, a Republican, and 2 third-party nominees, Clinton retains an average lead of 3.2% over Trump.

Based on the FiveThirtyEight website, which regularly updates their data, spots a 31.5% chance of winning for Trump compared to the former 30.9% possibility that Trump got.

Towards the election day, Clinton campaign team choose to be careful yet confident. For them, Trump winning the Presidential position would need to be viewed as an unassuming shocked.

ELECTION NIGHT

Trump's manager Kellyanne Conway and transition team leader Chris Christie were at the New York Hilton Midtown to pre-celebrate with the Republican supporters as the night of vote tallying went on. The venue was packed with the Republican nominee's supporters. Among present was known Celebrity supporter Stephen Baldwin, the crowd looked like they were already celebrating even before the initial results went in. As more results went in, it already became evident that a Republican nominee had bagged the position as the President.

Not far away was Clinton's campaign team who choose to gather at Javits Center. As the night of tallying went on the Clinton supporters grew anxiously, and then the tense feeling quickly turned into a heartbreak as it became evident that the party no longer on the running for the Presidential position. It came to a point that Podesta, the Democratic campaign chairman came out and convince the crowd to rest and head home, leaving them a promise that Clinton will appear days later to deliver her speech.

Many were surprised as a more detailed tally was released, showing that the Democratic candidate lost where she believes she had the advantage. These states include Pennsylvania, Michigan, and

Wisconsin. As John Podestra said: "They're still counting votes and every vote should count. Several states are too close to call, so we're not gonna have anything more to say tonight," as he was trying to comfort the supports. But a few minutes following this statement Trump received a call from Clinton, to express that she had conceded. According to sources, Clinton was urged by the Obama saying in a phone conversation "You need to concede." The Obama call was controversial as claimed by some Clinton supporters who believed that the Secretary of State should have waited a few more hours for the official announcement.

However, Clinton was keen on acknowledging her loss and said: "I'm calling him," then again insisted saying "Just give me the phone."

The Green Party head Jill Stein, pushed for a recount and Clinton's camp was having second thoughts on joining Stein. Apparently, Clinton's camp and the White House does not share the same sentiments with regards to the recount. However, days following the event the Clinton campaign team supported the Green Party and proposed to launch a recount particularly on the ballots for states of Michigan, Wisconsin, and Pennsylvania.

The then presumptive President Trump had condemned the efforts for a recount stating: "Hilary Clinton conceded the election when she called me just prior to the victory speech and after the results were in." He also insisted on saying "Nothing will change."

ELECTION RESULTS WHICH STATES WENT FOR WHO

After millions of Americans have gone to the polls and voted we can now decide on a winner.

Once the votes had been tallied, it turned out to be apparent that surveys amid the campaign had failed to predict the situation.

Hillary Clinton's pre-election day lead faded away as Donald Trump cleared the board to topple the Democratic nominee. Essential states including Florida, Ohio, North Carolina and Pennsylvania filled for the disputable Republican.

It was a crushing loss for Clinton, who did not go to her campaign HQ following the results.

Trump Wins

Texas	(38 Electoral Votes)
Florida	(29 Electoral Votes)
Pennsylvania	(20 Electoral Votes)
Ohio	(18 Electoral votes)
Georgia	(16 Electoral Votes)
North Carolina	(15 Electoral votes)
Indiana	(11 Electoral Votes)
Tennessee	(11 Electoral Votes)
Missouri	(10 Electoral Votes)
Wisconsin	(10 Electoral Votes)
Alabama	(9 Electoral Votes)

Colorado   (9 Electoral Votes)
South Carolina   (9 Electoral Votes)
Kentucky   (8 Electoral Votes)
Louisiana   (8 Electoral Votes)
Oklahoma   (7 Electoral Votes)
Mississippi   (6 Electoral Votes)
Arkansas   (6 Electoral votes)
Kansas   (6 Electoral Votes)
Utah   (6 Electoral Votes)
Iowa   (6 Electoral Votes)
West Virginia   (5 Electoral Votes)
Nebraska   (5 Electoral Votes)
Idaho   (4 Electoral Votes)
Montana   (3 Electoral Votes)
North Dakota   (3 Electoral Votes)
South Dakota   (3 Electoral Votes)
Wyoming   (3 Electoral Votes)

Clinton Wins

California   (55 Electoral Votes)
New York   (29 Electoral Votes)
Illinois   (20 Electoral Votes)
New Jersey   (14 Electoral Votes)
Virginia   (13 Electoral Votes)
Washington   (12 Electoral Votes)
Massachusetts   (11 Electoral Votes)
Maryland   (10 Electoral Votes)
Colorado   (9 Electoral Votes)
Oregon   (7 Electoral Votes)
Connecticut   (7 Electoral Votes)
Nevada   (6 Electoral Votes)
New Mexico   (5 Electoral Votes)

Max Vanguard

Hawaii   (4 Electoral Votes)
Rhode Island   (4 Electoral Votes)
Maine   (4 Electoral Votes)
Vermont   (3 Electoral Votes)
Delaware   (3 Electoral Votes)
DC   (3 Electoral Votes)

RIOTS IN STREETS

A number of people were not pleased with the election results, thousands of militants rally to the streets of New York Manhattan as they march towards the Trump Tower. People in thousands choose to gather at Manhattan park to show their dismay on Trump's victory as they shouted: "Not my president!"

According to the police report, an estimated 6,000 demonstrators were present and they were able to block traffic in Oakland, California. Militants burned trash in the middle of an intersection, a small group lit up fireworks, while other destroy storefront businesses. As some of the protesters hurled objects at the police, the police were forced to react by tossing chemical irritants, as told by witnesses.

In downtown Chicago, 1,800 gathered outside the Trump International Hotel and Tower while chanting phrases like: "No Trump! No KKK! No racist USA!"

The Chicago police closed roads in the area, as thousands gathered outside Tump International Hotel and Tower. However, there were no records found or immediate reports of an arrests or violence.

In Los Angeles, protesters sat on the 101 Hollywood Freeway, blocking traffic as police in riot gear watched. A 22-year-old protester was seen carrying a placard saying "Enjoy your rights while you can." The particular rally was joined by mostly high school and college students that are reported to have reached 5,000 in number.

Demonstrators also gathered in Seattle. There were initial reports of a shooting that allegedly had casualties, near the venue where the anti-Trump rally was held. However, police said that upon further investigation the shooting was not related to the rally being held that night.

Hundreds of America's youth also took part of the rally. Concerned young high school and college students walked out in protest in Seattle, Phoenix, Los Angeles and Oakland, Richmond and El Cerrito, California.

Protesters were furious about Trump's program that they considered being racist, along with the plan to build a wall at the Mexico border, to keep out undocumented immigrants.

Hundreds likewise rallied in Philadelphia and Boston. In Austin Texas, there were around 400 individuals who walked through the streets, as accounted by a police officer. The media were seeking for a reaction from the Republican camp but the Trump campaign was not keen on giving away any statements during the hype of the protest.

A Latino crowd of around 300 high school students stepped out of their classes in Los Angeles to show their support for the anti-Trump campaign. They were shouting "El pueblo unido nunca será derrotado" which in English means 'the people united will never be defeated', they were also seen carrying signs such as "Not Supporting Racism, Not My President" and "Immigrants Make America Great" printed on them as they walked towards the City Hall. The students held a wild yet brief rally.

Many of those students were members of the "Dreamers" generation, children whose parents entered the US with them unlawfully, school officials said, and who fear deportation under a Trump administration.

In his victory speech, Trump insisted that he would be a president for all Americans, saying: "It is time for us to come together as one united people." The Republican team also said, "Mr. Trump and his campaign denounces hate in any form".

EXPECTATION OF WHAT WILL FOLLOW

Chapter 6

TRUMP SUPREME COURT JUDGES

President-elect Donald Trump is that peculiar president who will likely assign a Supreme Court justice subsequently to taking office. He is expected to have a huge role in shaping the composition of the Supreme Court for the coming decades.

Following the death of Justice Antonin Scalia, who died in February, then President Obama called for Merrick Garland to replace Scalia's seat. However, the Senate Republicans refused to hold a hearing for Garland. This means handing the decision to incoming President Trump to fill at least one seat on the country's highest court.

During an interview with Sean Hannity, Trump stated he has narrowed down his original list of 21 people to "probably three or four." Trump said on Fox News Channel "They are terrific people, highly respected, brilliant people. We'll be announcing that pretty soon."

Among those who are also expected to leave the justice court and retire is 78-year-old Stephen Breyer and 83-year-old Ruth Bader Ginsburg.

The Republican candidate has shown bolster for exceptionally conservative judges. He said he needs to topple Roe v. Wade, the point of interest case giving women the privilege to abortion, and stated that the Court needs to "uphold the Second

Amendment."

Trump's rundown of candidates contains some surprising selections, for example, Utah Sen. Mike Lee. Generally, majority of Trump's potential candidates have a background in supporting conservative issues.

To date here are Donald Trump's potential Supreme Court nominees:

1. Keith Blackwell
2. Charles Canady
3. Steven Colloton
4. Allison Eid
5. Neil Gorsuch
6. Raymond Gruender
7. Thomas Hardiman
8. Raymond Kethledge
9. Joan Larsen
10. Mike Lee
11. Thomas Lee
12. Edward Mansfield
13. Federico Moreno
14. William Pryor
15. Margaret A. Ryan
16. Amul Thapar
17. Timothy Tymkovich
18. David Stras
19. Diane Sykes
20. Don Willett
21. Robert Young

REPLACE OBAMACARE

Congress returns to work a week after the election, and one of the priority is to look inside and strip Obamacare.

In order to replace the existing Obamacare, legislation would require 60 votes in the Senate, however, the Republicans do not have the strength in numbers to counter the Democrats seated in office.

Rather, Republican officials rely upon the gut key arrangements of the law utilizing the budget reconciliation process. This procedure is constrained to arrangements that influence government incomes and spending and requires just a simple majority to pass. It would empower Congress to remove the Obamacare. Additionally, it can get rid of the government subsidies, wipe out funding for Medicaid expansion and eliminate a significant number of Obamacare-related expenses.

Donald Trump's victory over Hillary Clinton predicts well for the future of America's healthcare system.

With Obamacare in an all out "downward spiral," voters were plainly in no condition for Clinton's proposal to "expand on" the president's health care law. Rather, they picked a president who has said that his first request of business will be to "ask Congress to quickly convey a full nullification of Obamacare."

According to President Obama and his partners, it's an open question. As he hands it over to the Clinton campaign rally days before the election, Obama stated that the Republicans "got no plan" to replace Obamacare.

However, under Speaker Paul Ryan's direction, House Republicans have put forth an alternate plan, and according to Ryan he described it as "A Better Way." He continued and maintained that the house is working on a more detailed health care plan compared to that of what Obama has off his sleeves. Ryan said that the system would run on an expanded coverage that guarantees to reduce expenses and also preserve those with existing health conditions.

Ryan said that as of the moment everything is still on paper. The next round is to work on an official legislation and then proceed with the federal cost estimates. Once executed, it promises to strengthen in places where Obamacare did not.

BUILDING A WALL ON MEXICAN BORDER

Donald Trump has always been put in hot water because of his policy regarding illegal immigrants and his illustrious talk on building a wall along the US-Mexico border.

The newly appointed Republican presidential Donald Trump ended his soft approach on immigration policies, during the campaign last September 2016 he said that he would deport undocumented immigrants living in the US and renewing his claim of having Mexico pay for the wall that he was planning to build along the border. Aiming at the citizenship for immigrants who were already in the U.S., Trump said: "There will be no amnesty!" "Mexico will pay for the wall 100%." Trump added, "They don't know it yet, but they're going to pay for the wall". To which the crowd responded shouting, "Build that wall!"

Trump claims the wall is necessary since the Mexico border is a gateway for illegal immigrants, criminals, and rapists' to come to the US.

But will the construction be underway soon? Will the Republican businessman follow through on this bold campaign promise?

The Mexican border wall was one of Mr. Trump's most eye-catching and outlandish policies.

According to the Department of Government at Exeter University's Dr. Gina Yannitell Reinhardt, it is "unlikely but not impossible" that Trump will be able to build the wall.

However, Dr. Reinhardt was quick to weigh in and said, "He needs a lot of money to do that. Congress does not support building the wall. It would be a very complicated endeavor."

Mexico has already made it clear that they will not fund the building of the wall. Nonetheless, Mexico asserted that they would keep their good relations with the US and will work with President-elect Trump for the benefit of both nations, but repeated that they would not pay for his planned border wall. Mexican President Peña Nieto even met with Mr. Trump in September and stated: "I made it clear that Mexico will not pay for the wall."

There are slim chances of Trump winning his battle with Congress as he seeks approval and funding for the construction project. Chances are that the Congress could block the plan in the Senate and House of Representatives.

Based on record there is already an existing 650 miles long wall out of the 2,000 miles long border, however, there were still reports that drug cartels constantly tunnel under it.

Trump has estimated the wall to cost roughly around $12 billion but fact shows that it could easily equal to double of Trump's calculation.

Spanish newspaper La Vanguardia said it is "unlikely" that we will see the construction of a wall between Mexico and the United States. The newspaper said, "In spite of the immense amount of money that the project would cost, its construction could give him grave problems with his Latin American neighbors and the rest of the world."

And even acknowledge that "it is not clear that Congress would support this initiative."

TRADE DEALS – RENEGOTIATE

Trade is one of the key issues during the election. And since America has now chosen a new President, United States is expected to experience a few changes on trade policies. It was reported that Trump had accused China and Mexico over stripping job opportunities from the US, in return the Republican candidate wants to impose high tariffs towards both countries.

The new administration is yet to announce their plan on trade, but based on Trump's statement towards China, we can somehow already see what's coming. Analysts say that US could resort to limiting imports of steel and aluminum from China into the U.S. with a goal to get control over a surge of low-quality metal imports that have had a huge impact on U.S. manufacturers.

Also, we can see that Trump will take a step towards strengthening its executive branch focusing on China's currency control. China is regularly attacked for fictitiously increasing the value of Yuan in a way that they can sell goods and services of cheaper value.

These activities would likely mean making an option for nations to settle trade issues, which the World Trade Organization administers. While the WTO principles are exceptionally important, they are two decades old and no longer fits the trend on what trade is today. Having recognized this the government under Trump's leadership is assumed to summon the president's unilateral trade authority as an influence on deciding some issues through proper negotiation.

The Trans-Atlantic Trade and Investment Partnership between the US and the European Union is likely on the backend of Trump's trade priorities. After United Kingdom had decided to leave EU, negotiations went slow and uncertain. Granting Trump's judgment towards free trade, it is likely that they will re-evaluate the existing trade agreements and the chances are that they are going to opt for an extended break before the Trump Administration chooses to hold a discussion on the so-called partnership.

But the Republican party has made it clear that they do not want to throw away the current trade agreement but insisted on making better agreements. However, they have not disclosed any information on which agreement applies to which country. Being that UK and US share the same sets of standards in terms of our products and services, UK would be a perfect choice to set-off renegotiations on trade agreements

To add to the list of renegotiation is NAFTA or the North American Free Trade Agreement. Trump still can't seem to explicitly indicate what's the downside of the agreement other than that it had a huge effect on U.S. employment. Currently, the new Administration is yet to decide on what steps to take, but sources say that they have already made efforts to set renegotiation talks.

According to the Constitution as President, the 70-year old businessman-politician has jurisdiction over the agreements, he can approve or forgo the agreement without Congress, this could only mean that the Countries involve will have no choice but to represent themselves at the negotiating table.

According to the Constitution as President, the 70-year old businessman-politician has jurisdiction over the agreements, he can approve or forgo the agreement without Congress, this could only mean that the Countries involve will have no choice but to represent themselves at the negotiating table.

REFERENCES

URL LINKS

http://www.foxnews.com/politics/2016/11/02/fbis-clinton-foundation-investigation-now-very-high-priority-sources-say.html

http://www.politico.com/magazine/story/2016/07/hillary-clinton-emails-history-214095

http://www.people-press.org/2016/08/18/clinton-trump-supporters-have-starkly-different-views-of-a-changing-nation/

https://www.nytimes.com/2016/10/02/us/politics/donald-trump-taxes.html

http://www.denverpost.com/2015/08/25/colorado-republicans-cancel-presidential-vote-at-2016-caucus/

http://www.newsday.com/opinion/oped/colorado-super-tuesday-rules-disenfranchise-most-voters-1.11525395

http://edition.cnn.com/2015/09/01/opinions/sexton-trump-carson-fiorina-outsiders/

http://www.ranker.com/list/2016-presidential-candidates-controversies/ranker-news

http://2016.republican-candidates.org/

http://2016.democratic-candidates.org/

http://www.news.com.au/finance/work/leaders/do-super-delegates-rig-the-democratic-primaries-in-hillary-clintons-favour/news-story/590348429e8eb7fcbee22961c2a909aa

https://www.washingtonpost.com/news/post-politics/wp/2016/06/06/in-a-tense-exchange-bernie-sanders-says-his-refusal-to-quit-is-not-sexist/?utm_term=.e1e5e3fbb07b

https://www.hiiraan.com/news4/2016/Sept/117880/clinton_stays_calm_while_trump_loses_cool_during_first_presidential_debate.aspx

http://fortune.com/2016/10/09/heres-who-won-the-second-presidential-debate/

POLITICS OF CLINTON AND TRUMP

http://learningenglish.voanews.com/a/us-vice-presidential-candidates-debate-policies-of-trump-and-clinton/3538045.html

https://www.forbes.com/sites/vickyvalet/2016/09/25/hillary-clinton-vs-donald-trump-where-the-candidates-stand-on-employment-and-jobs/#66aa9b835e55

http://www.wsj.com/graphics/elections/2016/donald-trump-hillary-clinton-on-social-issues/

http://www.aljazeera.com/programmes/listeningpost/2016/10/wikileaks-political-hacks-election-161023102730794.html

https://www.nytimes.com/2016/10/02/us/politics/donald-trump-taxes.html?_r=0

http://www.foxnews.com/entertainment/2016/10/18/nbc-news-fires-billy-bush-after-lewd-donald-trump-tape-airs.html

http://www.latimes.com/nation/politics/trailguide/la-na-trailguide-updates-reluctant-trump-supporter-paul-ryan-1475907609-htmlstory.html

http://fortune.com/2016/08/21/millenials-dont-like-donald-trump-or-hillary-clinton/

http://www.politico.com/story/2016/10/donald-trump-bill-clinton-accusers-229441

http://www.thedailybeast.com/articles/2016/10/12/all-of-donald-trump-s-accusers-a-timeline-of-every-alleged-grope-and-assault.html

http://www.aljazeera.com/blogs/americas/2016/11/hillary-clinton-donald-trump-rallies-161104233413813.html

http://rightwingnews.com/hillary-clinton-2/hillarys-doctor-releases-diagnosis-video/

http://www.foxnews.com/politics/2016/10/12/bias-alert-wikileaks-exposes-medias-secret-support-clinton.html

http://www.foxnews.com/politics/2016/10/11/republicans-claim-

Max Vanguard

collusion-after-email-appears-to-show-doj-clinton-campaign-contact.html

http://www.mirror.co.uk/news/world-news/who-winning-election-2016-results-922177

http://www.businessinsider.com/president-elect-donald-trump-supreme-court-list

http://www.express.co.uk/news/politics/730583/Donald-Trump-will-US-President-build-wall-border-Mexico-America-Mexican-illegal-immigrants

https://en.wikipedia.org/wiki/United_States_presidential_election,_2016

https://en.wikipedia.org/wiki/Results_of_the_Democratic_Party_presidential_primaries,_2016

http://www.justfacts.com/globalwarming.asp

http://www.cnn.com/2016/07/05/politics/fbi-director-doesnt-recommend-charges-against-hillary-clinton/

http://www.cnbc.com/2016/07/07/rep-trey-gowdy-rips-into-fbi-director-james-comey-on-hillary-clintons-intent.html

http://www.epi.org/blog/naftas-impact-workers/

https://www.scientificamerican.com/article/sun-spots-and-climate-change/

http://www.cnsnews.com/news/article/susan-jones/clinton-explains-why-she-said-one-thing-chelsea-something-else-benghazi

https://www.thenewamerican.com/usnews/crime/item/23532-benghazi-probe-obama-officials-refused-to-address-gun-running

http://www.nationalreview.com/article/430153/fast-furious-obama-first-scandal
http://www.kiplinger.com/article/taxes/T056-C000-S001-where-clinton-and-trump-stand-on-taxes.html

http://www.washingtontimes.com/news/2016/oct/12/top-10-hillary-

POLITICS OF CLINTON AND TRUMP

clinton-scandals-exposed-wikileaks/

http://www.politifact.com/punditfact/statements/2017/jan/06/jesse-watters/claim-john-podestas-email-password-was-password-la/

http://dailycaller.com/2017/03/15/justice-department-sued-for-records-about-lynchs-tarmac-meeting-with-clinton/

Max Vanguard

TRUMP BUSINESS

Book 2

INTRODUCTION

Chapter 1

Empire of Donald Trump. Throughout this book, we are going to explore the business empire of Donald J. Trump. From his early years, all the way to his 2016 presidential victory, we will discover just what has led to this man's success.

In recent years, Donald J. Trump has become the face of many magazines, the topic of many articles, and the name in many headlines. Despite always having experienced a fair level of fame, his recent presidential campaign has truly resulted in his name and face being plastered across the American nation. His campaign has led to the interest of many, with people wondering where he came from, how he built his empire, and why he is so successful.

The reality is, Trump has been well-known for years due to his various endeavors in the business world. His most memorable business endeavor is his incredibly successful real estate business. In addition to that, he has also been involved in several other ventures that have all contributed to the Trump brand's success. From his various appearances on famous television shows and networks to his famous real estate business, and his two presidential campaigns, Trump has been involved in just about every level of corporate America. Despite him being a part of several failed business ventures, Trump has devised the perfect empire for himself and has been responsible for the success of his career, as well as his brand and many of his businesses.

In this book, we are going to explore how Trump's early years and basic education contributed to the creation of his empire. We are also going to explore some of the many business ventures Trump has embarked on throughout his history as a famous businessman, including all of his failures and some of his best successes. This book will help you discover how his personal life has contributed to his success, and how his commitment to and affection for business has led to his multi-billion-dollar business empire. We will even explore the topic of Trump's presidential campaign, and what he did to win the election despite not having any significant political experience. This book is geared towards teaching you about the extensive history of Trump and his business empire, and the unpredictable but likely successful future it faces. If you are interested in learning more about this successful businessman, TV reality show host and film cameo, and 45th President of the United States, then you have purchased the right book for you.

Max Vanguard

THE START OF AN EMPIRE

Chapter 2

While Donald Trump played a major role in the development of his business empire, there was a significant number of factors from his early life that can be attributed to his overall success. He was born to successful parents who came from a successful lineage, particularly in the real estate industry. He was adopted into the family business in his young adult years and taught the ropes by his father, who was originally taught by his mother, or Donald's grandmother. There are many reasons why Trump managed to make such a successful rise to business fame, and while his own efforts and strategies are largely responsible for his victories, his early life is just as important in his achievement of success. Trump's keen discipline started as young as his high school years when the extremely energetic young man was moved to a new school by his father to help promote a more positive release for his energy. From the very beginning, with the help of his parents and family, Trump was destined for success in the world of business. In this chapter, we are going to explore deeper into the life of Donald Trump, and how his earliest years on Earth were spent priming him for the success and victories, he would achieve later in life.

Growing Up

Donald J. Trump was born on June 14, 1946, to his father, Fred Trump, and his mother, Mary Trump. His parents raised him and his four siblings in a neighborhood known as Jamaica, Queens, New York City. Donald was the fourth child to be born to his parents, he had two brothers and two sisters. In 1981, Donald's older brother, Fred Jr, died from alcoholism. After experiencing the loss of his brother due to his addiction, Donald has decided to remain abstinent from alcohol and cigarettes and has done so for the majority of his life.

Donald is born to a combination of Germanic and Scottish ancestry. Both his paternal German grandparents and his maternal Scottish grandparents were born in Europe, though his parents met in New York. His father, like Donald, was also born in Queens, New York. On the other hand, his mother was born in Lewis, Scotland but later emigrated to New York. It was after her emigration that she met Donald's father. His parents married in 1936 and established their household in Queens where they raised their five children, including Donald and his four brothers and sisters.

Donald was born into a long line of successful family members. Outside of the family real estate business, there were other members of his family who had become incredibly successful in their respective lines of work. In particular, he had an uncle named John Trump who was a professor at the Massachusetts Institute of Technology. John Trump also assisted the Allies of World War II by conducting radar research. The same uncle was also involved in developing x-ray machines that were responsible for providing additional years of life for cancer patients. When Nikola Tesla died in his hotel room, it was John Trump who was requested to examine Tesla's papers by the Federal Bureau of Investigation. In addition to his successful uncle, Donald also had a successful grandfather, Frederick Trump. Frederick created his success through establishing and operating boom-town restaurants and boarding houses. His businesses, which were located in Seattle and Klondike, Canada, were responsible for his fortune.

On Donald's paternal side, his grandfather was the owner of a middle-class real estate business based in New York. When his grandfather died, his grandmother took over the business and renamed it "Elizabeth Trump & Son" and maintained it for the sake of her family. Donald's father helped his grandmother run the business, and eventually, his grandmother retired and later passed away. When Trump was old enough, the family business was his first entry into the world of real estate. It was also the foundation upon which he built his entire business empire. While many people believe that Trump was the product of his father's fortunes, the reality is that he and his father built the empire together, and when his father passed away, he left a large portion of his share to Donald. While his father's fortune certainly acted as leverage to further Trump's business empire, it was not the basis upon which his empire was built.

Education

Donald Trump's earliest education experience was in The Kew-Forest School, which he attended until he was 13 years old. While he attended this school, he lived in Queens with the other 6 members of his family in a modest, two-story home. When Donald turned 13 years old, his parents transferred him out of The Kew-Forest School and into the New York Military Academy (NYMA). There, Donald finished the remaining 5 years of his high school education. Trump's parents had decided to enroll him in the academy in hopes that they would be able to teach him discipline and help him focus his enormous amounts of energy into something positive. By his senior year at NYMA, Trump had climbed the ranks and earned himself the position as captain. However, he was allegedly in charge of the barracks that were involved in the hazing of a new freshman, which resulted in him being transferred to a student command position. Trump recalls this transfer as a promotion of his ranks and does not regret the transfer.

Trump's post-secondary education began in August 1964 at Fordham University, which is located in the Bronx. After studying there for two years, he transferred to The Wharton School of the University of Pennsylvania, in Philadelphia, USA. The Wharton School became a family legacy, as two of his own children later attended the same school for the same studies as Donald, himself. At the time Donald attended, this university was one of the few to offer a department on real estate studies in all of the United States of America. He completed his Bachelor of Science degree in Economics and graduated from the University in May 1968.

Although he has enlisted in the military largely thanks to his involvement in the NYMA, Trump was never drafted for the Vietnam war. During his time in college, between the years of 1964 and 1968, Trump obtained four student deferments which kept him from being drafted. He was deemed fit for service in both 1966 and 1968 from military medical examinations, but in October 1968 had his classification revoked as they gave him a 1-Y medical deferment. In an interview in 2015, Trump claimed this deferment was the result of heel spurs. Luck stayed in his corner, however, because in December of 1969, Trump dodged the draft again during the draft lottery. Donald drew a high number, which meant he was not required to provide his services to the military. This allowed him to stay out of military action and focus his energy on the family business and working alongside his father to build the basis of the family's empire.

Entry into Family Business

As previously stated, Trump's entry into the real estate business began before he ever graduated from university. Trump began his business with a real estate career at his family company, Elizabeth Trump, and Son, which was now being operated by his father. The company was named after his grandmother on his father's side. At the time, it was focused on dealing with New York real estate, primarily in the boroughs of Queens, Brooklyn, and Staten Island. They were involved in the real estate investments of middle-classed rental housing units.

While Trump was working on his undergraduate study, he and his father used a $500,000 investment which was the first move in expanding their business outside of New York City. The investment was used to reopen the Swifton Village apartment complex, which had been foreclosed. The Cincinnati, Ohio complex investment proved to be a major success for the company and opened doors for them to continue expanding their business across the United States.

In 1971, Trump was awarded control over the family real estate company by his father. One of his first orders of business was to rename the establishment to "The Trump Organization," which allowed for him to expand the organization's abilities and increase the amount of business they could operate under its title. Two years following his overtaking of the company, he became the official president of the organization. During that same year, in 1973, Trump and his father attracted enormous amounts of media attention to their business through an alleged case of racial discrimination. It was reported that two had allegedly been involved in discrimination against blacks who were attempting to rent their apartments. The Trump father and son duo claimed to be screening people out based on low income, but reports stated that the two had been basing their decisions on race. Sometime after the allegations were made and the case was brought up in court, the Trump father and son duo signed an agreement. In the agreement, the two never admitted to doing anything wrong. In addition to their lack of admission, they agreed to qualify minority applicants that were presented by the Urban League, which is a civil rights organization responsible for advocating on behalf of African Americans. The agreement meant that they would be forced to offer equal opportunities to African Americans as they were to white America. This agreement also removed their case from the public eye and allowed for them to carry on with business.

From this early start in Trump's career, with the help of his father and the family business, Trump was able to go on to build an entire empire. He established his firm roots in New York City, and eventually went on to expand his real estate business operations beyond New York and into several other areas of the United States and, eventually, across the globe. He continues to hold a large amount of real estate in New York, including the original Trump Tower which features his penthouse home that he lives in with his current wife and youngest son.

The expansion of Trump's real estate empire allowed for him to branch out into several other areas of business, including various endeavors from alcohol production, to television involvement. He was also able to use his broad business title to adopt his eldest children into the empire and allow for them to use the brand and company to establish their successful roots in business and carry on to build their own empires. Trump went from a small, New York City-based, middle-class real estate business, to a full-on luxurious real estate empire, several other branches of business, and eventually a presidential victory in his 50 years of business. All of his success can largely be attributed to his foundation, which was formed by his family business, and his diligent parents who encouraged him to establish strong discipline and focus his energy on positive goals.

FAMILY LIFE

Chapter 3

Trump's family has always been a major part of the famous businessman's success. From his earliest years, all the way until his most recent victories, he has always kept his family involved in his successes. While his parents are no longer a part of the picture, Trump continues to share his successes and business endeavors with his children and spouses. Trump's love for business has meant that his wives have had to be committed to his business as well. In fact, he believes his first two marriages failed due to his wives' lack of ability to understand his affection and commitment to the business. It is also likely that this understanding is the same reason why his current marriage to Melania Trump has been so successful: she has been able to maintain a strong level of involvement in his business endeavors, while also staying back and helping raise their son and allowing for Trump to chase his goals.

Trumps family currently consists of two ex-wives with whom he has a combination of four children, his current wife with whom he has one son, and eight grandchildren. He also has several extended family members who are an important part of his life, as well. His family has been an incredible part of his success, both in life and in business. Many have contributed in his business functions, including three of his children who are currently in charge of The Trump Organization.

Wives

Trump has been married a total of three times, meaning he now has two ex-wives, and his current wife: Melania. Each time he was married, he had at least one child with his wife, leaving him with a total of five children. Throughout his previous two marriages, Trump always felt that his wives' were incapable of understanding his affection and love for business, and became jealous over his dedication to his career. He feels that this was the reason why both marriages failed, and it is likely also the same reason why his marriage to Melania has been a success so far. Trump's wives have held important roles in his business, including promoting his companies, contributing to the success of business relationships, overseeing the operations of various Trump businesses, and more recently, contributing to his presidential campaign and victory.

His first wife was Ivana Zeinickova, whom he married on April 17, 1977. While he was married to Ivana, she gave birth to Donald's three eldest children. These children, in order, included: Donald Trump Jr., Ivanka Trump, and Eric Trump. The wedding between Donald and Ivana was held at the Marble Collegiate Church, which is located in Manhattan. Their wedding ceremony was performed by Reverend Norman Vincent Peale, who is regarded as one of the most famous wedding ministers in the United States. In addition to being Trump's wife, Ivana Zeinickova served as one of Trump's partners in business. Zeinickova took over the responsibility for overseeing the management and operations of several of Trump's business endeavors, including the Plaza Hotel in Manhattan, New York.

Trump and Zeinickova remained married for 15 years, though the final three years of their marriage was rocky. Following hardships in their marriage, Trump began having an affair with the American actress, Marla Maples. The affair began being reported by the tabloids in 1990 and continued to be reported for the following two years. Because of the affair, Trump and Zeinickova were able to file for a quick divorce, and the marriage was ultimately terminated in 1992. Despite the failed marriage and legal issues that followed it, 23 years later when Trump was running for president, Zeinickova made a statement claiming she and Trump are "the best of friends."

The affair with Marla Maples didn't turn out to be a total waste of time, despite the fact that it destroyed his previous marriage to the mother of his first three children. Quickly after the termination of his first marriage, Maples discovered she was pregnant with Trump's child. In 1993, she gave birth to Trump's fourth child, and second daughter, Tiffany Trump. Tiffany was named after the famous New York location of the jewelry store "Tiffany & Company." The name came about because Trump's Tower on Fifth Avenue, New York, was built above this jewelry store after Trump purchased the air space above it and built his tower in the 1980s. Two months after the birth of their daughter, Trump and Maples officially tied the knot. Their wedding date was on December 20, 1993. While the marriage was short-lived at only six years long, it gave an incredible amount of exposure and publicity to the actress and helped launch her career into greater success. In 1997, the couple officially separated, and in 1999 they finalized their divorce.

In 1998, following his separation from Maples but before the finalizing of their divorce, Trump began dating his now-wife, Melania Knauss. Trump dated the Slovane fashion model for six years before asking her to marry him in April of 2004. Their engagement was less than a year long, as they officially wed on January 22, 2005. Trump and Melania were married in Palm Beach, Florida, at the Bethesda-by-the-Sea Episcopal Church. Following their vows, they hosted their wedding reception party at Trump's Mar-a-Lago estate, which is also located in Palm Beach.

Melania became an official citizen of the United States about a year after the two married, in 2006. Later that same year, Melania gave birth to Trump's fifth child and third son: Barron Trump. Due to having been raised in a household with regular usage of both Slovene and English, Barron was raised naturally bilingual, with a fluent ability to speak both languages. Donald and Melania's marriage remains successful and strong, and Donald largely attributes that to Melania's ability to understand and respect his affection for his career. In fact, Melania even played a role in Donald's presidential campaign of 2015-16, despite the controversy that arose over his many derogatory, sexist and perverted remarks. In one interview, she claimed that his words were being twisted and that despite the media and nation's dislike towards her husband, she remained supportive and loving towards Donald and his endeavor.

Children

From his three separate marriages, Trump has been gifted with five children. His first marriage resulted in the birth of his three eldest children, followed by his second marriage which resulted in the birth of his fourth child, and his third marriage which has led to the birth of his fifth and youngest child. These children, like his wives, have had a profound impact on his business endeavors. Particularly his eldest children, who have each completed their university degrees and have begun their work with the family company, as well as some of their own ventures. Following his presidential victory in November of 2016, Trump announced that he was turning the responsibility of his business, The Trump Organization, over to his eldest children who would continue to oversee the success and growth of the company. This occurred due to the legality of the situation, and his inability to maintain any say over the company due to conflict of interest.

His first child, Donald Trump Jr., was born the same year that his first marriage took place: 1977. He is the eldest of Trump's children and was 15 years old when his parents divorced. Unlike his younger siblings, Donald Jr. was old enough to understand the nasty headlines circulating about his father's affair when he was just 12 years old, which meant his peers were also understanding of the situation and some even passed judgment on Donald Jr., bullying him for his father's actions. He watched the media attack his father and his father's affair for three years before the divorce was finalized. Donald Jr. maintained a close relationship with his maternal grandfather until his grandfather's passing in 1990. The two often spent many weeks together, fishing and enjoying the outdoors. Donald Jr. faced a bit of an egotistical streak in college, where he was noted for drinking often and getting in fights on the basis of "do-you-know-who-I-am?." He took a year off after his college graduation, and then Donald Jr. followed in his father's footsteps by taking on a position in the family company in 2001. Now, in 2016, Donald Jr. holds the position of executive vice president of The Trump Organization.

Donald Jr. met his wife Vanessa at a fashion show where the date was arranged by his father, Donald Sr. He later publicly proposed to his now-wife in front of a jewelry store, with the presence of several photographers to snap the happy moment. Many rumors circulated about the nature of the proposal, claiming it was a publicity stunt and Donald Jr. received the ring in trade for the exposure it gave the jewelry business. Regardless, the two have given birth to five children in their seven years together, which quickly lead to the burial of the rumors surrounding their engagement.

Trump's second child, Ivanka Trump, was another child born to his first wife, Ivana. Unlike the rest of her family who deals primarily in real estate, Ivanka has taken on a different route in business. In the same year as her brothers' acquiring o the Trump Hotel Collections, Ivanka launched her very own jewelry brand. The brand has evolved to include clothing, shoes, and various other accessories. She even has a small collection of shoes for babies. Her line can be found in some of the most popular fashion stores, including Nordstroms, Zappos, and Bloomingdales. Her own fashion business was her first step into the business world, despite it being off-track from what her family likely had planned for Ivanka. Regardless, the venture has proven to be successful, as her fashion collection is constantly growing and adding new lines each year. She has even assisted her younger sister, Tiffany, in launching her own fashion career.

Prior to her business launch, Ivanka had attended one of the same Universities as her father: The Wharton School. While she worked a brief gig in real estate with the developer Bruce Ratner, she ended that career after a year and moved forward with her fashion venture. Ivanka joined her father's company in 2005, working one time as the lead negotiator of Trump National Doral Miami. The tower was purchased for $150 million and is now worth an impressive $1 billion. While she is private about her personal life, it is known that Ivanka is now in her second marriage, where she is wed to Jared Kushner. The two live in the $16 million penthouse of Trump Park Avenue with their two children.

The third and final child Trump had with his first wife, Ivana, was Eric Trump. Eric remained a media-shy, baby of the family figure for a long time before emerging into the spotlight with the rest of his family. At one time, he told New York Magazine that his older brother (Donald Jr.) was like his mentor, and his older sister (Ivanka) was like his second mother. In the magazine, he was quoted saying: "She took me under her wing, raised me, took me shopping, tried to make me cool." Unlike his older siblings, Eric opted to go to Georgetown University, instead of Wharton. Following his graduation, he immediately took on a position with his family's company, holding a similar position as his sister, Ivanka. Eric serves as the executive vice president of acquisitions and development (the same title as Ivanka), but his focus is in construction, not acquiring businesses. Eric proposed to his then-girlfriend in 2012, following five years of dating. They were wed in front of 400 guests. The wedding ceremony took place at the Mar-a-Lago Club, located in Palm Beach, Florida.

Trump's fourth child and second daughter, Tiffany, was born by Marla Maples. She was raised significantly different than her older half-siblings, as she did not spend her childhood in her father's offices or in any of his many luxurious real estate holdings. Instead, Tiffany was raised in Calabasas, California, by Marla Maples. There, she attended a $31,205-a-year school called Viewpoint School. Tiffany is currently studying at the University of Pennsylvania and aspires to follow in her sister's footsteps and emerge into the fashion industry with her own business. It is reported that her older sister, Ivanka, helped Tiffany acquire her internship with Vogue, and in 2011 Tiffany released a single for her debut song. She is currently enjoying her youthful years by partying with "The Rich Kids of Instagram" and stars from the "Rich Kids of Beverly Hills" show. She enjoys traveling and often uses her father's private jet to get from place to place.

The fifth and final Trump child is his third son, Barron, born by Melania. Based on Melania's many descriptions of their son, it is believed that he may be more like Donald Sr. than any of his four older siblings. At just 9 years old in the year 2016, the young boy claims to prefer suits over sweatpants. He has his very own floor in his parents' Trump Tower penthouse, instead of just a bedroom like most children. The young Trump is said to enjoy baseball and tennis but has a special interest in golf, which is also his father's favorite sport. Due to his young age, Donald Sr. and Melania does their best to keep Barron out of the public eye as much as they can, but is lightly involved in some of the socialite events that his parents attend. One he has attended each year with his mother, Melania, in the Upper East Side of New York is one of the most popular children's social of the year, called the "Memorial-Sloan Kettering Bunny Hop."

LUXURIOS REAL ESTATE

Chapter 4

Real estate offered Trump his entry into the business world. It was the focus of his post-secondary education studies, as well as the basis of the family business he took over. Naturally, real estate continues to be one of the strongest pillars of Trump's success and continues to be the primary investment of The Trump Organization. Trump and his father took the family business from a New York-based company and pushed it further into the United States. However, Trump took that business and pushed it to be a leading global luxury real estate business. His business in real estate has led to his investment in several Towers consisting of luxurious, and expensive, condominiums, as well as various hotels and resorts, and several other real estate holdings across the world.

From Middle-Class to Luxurious Real Estate

The evolution of Trump's family business transitioning from middle-class to luxurious real estate began shortly after Trump joined the family business. He and his father made a monumental $500,000 investment in a foreclosed complex that paved the way for all of their future endeavors. The further they spread into the United States, the more successful the company became. The more successful the company became, the further they pushed, and the higher quality their investments became. Trump has continued to pursue the luxurious real estate business and has completely altered the face of his family's company. What was once a simple, yet successful one-state company has now become the global face of luxury real estate.

This portion of his endeavors built the majority of his successful business empire and is largely responsible for the victories Trump has faced. It continues to be the basis for his company today, with his three children overseeing the acquisition, development, and profitability of all new properties being handled by The Trump Organization.

Manhatten

In 1978, Trump made his first big deal in Manhattan real estate. This deal consisted of his company remodeling the Grand Hyatt Hotel, which was received a large majority of its funding by his father and the Hyatt hotel chain. In that same year, Trump completed the negotiations to build the Trump Tower. This tower was a 58-story, 208-meter tall skyscraper located in Manhattan, New York. In 1983, the Trump Tower's building was completed. The building continues to house the headquarters of The Trump Organization. It also serves as Donald Trump's primary place of residence, where he currently lives with Melania and Barron. In addition, the tower also gave home to NBC's television show *The Apprentice* (see: Chapter 6), which was filmed in the tower's very own fully-functional television studio set.

In 1986, Trump took over a project to repair an ice arena in Central Park. The Wollman Rink, which was built in 1955, had originally started the repairs in 1980 with a general contractor. The intention was for the project to be completed with a 2 ½ year completion schedule, but the project remained incomplete up until Trump took over. When he took over, the project was complete in three months. The total cost of reparation was $1.95 million, $750,000 less than what the initial budget was set for. With thanks to the $750,000 savings, the rink operated as a non-profit charity for one entire year. Meaning, all profits were donated to various charities during that calendar year, in return for the rink's concession rights.

In 1988, Trump paid $400 million for the Plaza Hotel in Manhattan. He renovated this hotel and continued its operations which contributed to a great deal of his business wealth. His wife, Ivana Trump, was hired to manage the operation and renovation of the hotel.

Palm Beach

In 1985, Trump expanded his business from New York to Palm Beach, Florida. There, he purchased the historical Mar-a-Lago estate. He paid a total of $8 million for the home, including all of its furnishings. This home was turned into a private club with $150,000 annual membership fees. He also uses the location as a private winter retreat for him and his family. Around the same time of his acquisition, Trump also purchased a condominium complex. The complex, located in Palm Beach, was purchased with Lee Lacocca, a business partner. This condominium was named the Trump Plaza.

Atlantic City

In 1984, Trump moved into the casino business. His first venture was with Harrah's at Trump Plaza, located in Atlantic City: it the first casino and hotel owned by Trump and was financed by Holiday Corp. The day-to-day workings were operated by the Holiday Corp's Harrah gambling unit. Despite what the team had hoped, the Trump Plaza was a flop, which led to extensive disagreements between the partners: Trump and the Holiday Corp. From there, Trump went on to acquire a partially completed building in Atlantic City, which he got from the Hilton Corporation. He paid a total of $320 million for the building and had it completed by 1985. Upon its completion, the hotel and casino became the Trump Castle. Once again, Ivana Trump was responsible for property management.

During 1988, Trump's company took the step of purchasing the Taj Mahal Casino, also in Atlantic City. The transaction took place between Trump and Merv Griffin, as well as Resorts International. In April 1990, the casino was opened with the total building cost of $1.1 billion. At the time of it's the Trump Taj Mahal was the most expensive casino ever to be built. The building's completion required financing of $675 million, acquired through junk bonds (a high-yield bond) with an interest rate of 14%. In the following year, 1991, the casino entered Chapter 11 bankruptcy. Due to the bankruptcy filing, all banks and bondholders who had invested in the business were facing major losses. Instead of incurring the losses, they chose to restructure the debt.

On October 5, 1991, the Taj Mahal Casino emerged from bankruptcy. In order to do so, Trump was forced to reduce to just 50% ownership. The rest was given to bondholders, which resulted in Trump having lowered interest rates on his debts, and a longer term to pay off the remaining balance. In the same year, Trump sold his failed airline business and plane (the Trump Princess). The property was then repurchased by The Trump Organization in 1996. Following the repurchase, The Trump Organization consolidated the location into Trump Hotels & Casino Resorts. In 2004, that company filed for bankruptcy with an astonishing $1.8 billion worth of debt. Five years later, he filed the same company for bankruptcy once again. This second bankruptcy was filed with $500 million in debt and $50 million in assets. Trump was left with just 10% ownership over his casinos following the restructuring that was required to reemerge from bankruptcy once again. In that company, which was renamed Trump Entertainment Resorts, Trump served as chairman of the organization. His position took place from mid-1995 until early 2009, during that time he also served as it's CEO. His position as CEO took place from mid-2000 to mid-2005.

Luxury Real Estate Holdings

The development of Trump's real estate business was a major contribution to his success in the business world. Trump's development of the real estate company "Trump International Realty," a daughter company to The Trump Organization, has enabled him to expand his real estate business even further and has been responsible for many major Trump real estate holdings across the globe. For the most part, Trump's business is involved in developing luxurious "condominium hotels" that are rented out for impressive prices and return massive amounts of revenue each year.

Trump's current real estate holdings include 32 different skyscrapers that are located across North America. Some of the most popular Trump buildings that can be found in the United States include Trump Tower on Fifth Avenue in New York, The Estate at Trump National, Trump International Hotel in Las Vegas, Trump Hollywood and Trump Park Residences and the Trump International Hotel and Tower in Chicago Illinois. In addition to his many towers and businesses across the United States, Trump has 8 towers that are located across the rest of the world. This number continues to grow each year, as the company continues to acquire more real estate holdings and develop the luxurious Trump buildings. The 8 towers that are located around the globe include two Trump Towers in India, one in Prune and one in Mumbai. He also has a Trump Tower in Makati, Philippines, and a Trump Ocean Club in Panama. His other four Trump Towers are located in Toronto, Ontario, and Vancouver, B.C in Canada, as well as one in Istanbul, Sisli, and one in Punta Del Este, Uruguay. Each tower that Trump's businesses have established across the world are worth millions, often even billions of dollars, and are highly successful businesses. These towers and resorts earn enormous amounts of revenue each year and are a large part of the successful business that is Trump's empire.

BANKCRUPTCIES

Chapter 5

In addition to several successful, multi-million-dollar business ventures, Trump has faced many failures in his businesses. Several times, Trump has entered bankruptcy with his endeavors. These bankruptcies, however, never managed to cripple even part of his company, and had no impact on Trump's success in the business world. In fact, Trump has suggested that he uses bankruptcy as a strategic part of his business in order to reduce the amount of money he must put into each business. First, he acquires a company with an initial set of negotiations, then he enters the company into Chapter 11 bankruptcy and negotiates a secondary set of terms which ultimately reduce his interest rates and give him a longer window of opportunity to pay back what he owes. While the strategy often costs him a large percentage of ownership in his companies, it also means that his percentage is easier to pay back and that he can carry on to other ventures.

Bankruptcies

Trump has filed for Chapter 11 bankruptcy with his companies a total of seven times. This form of bankruptcy allows for businesses to continue regular operations while formal re-negotiations are in process. Despite his many bankruptcies filed by his companies, Trump has never filed for personal bankruptcy. As we discovered in the previous chapter, the first time Trump filed for bankruptcy was with his Trump Taj Mahal Casino in Atlantic City, followed by many of his other casino companies. The three bankruptcies among his casino businesses resulted in major capital losses, as well as company ownership losses as they reduced Trump to a mere 10% of ownership in all of his Trump Casino properties.

Each time Trump's companies entered bankruptcy, Trump re-negotiated his debt with the banks and the owners of his stocks and bonds. In 2011, *Newsweek* reported with quoting Trump saying: "I do play with the bankruptcy laws – they're very good for me," ultimately stating that he used them as a tool for minimizing his debt. That being said, it's hard to view Trump's corporate bankruptcies as a failure if he was purposefully using them as an opportunity for him to enter into what he would consider a more desirable agreement.

The seven total bankruptcies spanned between Atlantic City and New York. The companies that filed for Chapter 11 bankruptcy include: Trump Taj Mahal Casino (filed in 1991), Trump Plaza Hotel and Casino, Plaza Hotel (filed in 1992), Trump Castle Hotel and Casino (filed in 1992), Trump Hotels and Casino Resorts (filed in 2004), and Trump Entertainment Resorts (filed in 2009, and again in 2014.) In regards to all of his bankruptcies, Trump has been quoted saying "I've used the laws of this country to pare debt ... We'll have the company. We'll throw it into a chapter. We'll negotiate it with the banks. We'll make a fantastic deal. You know, it's like on *The Apprentice*. It's not personal. It's just business." This stance has led to Trump having less ownership over his companies, but more freedom to expand into other ventures. Ultimately, it is hard to decipher whether the bankruptcies could be considered failure, or success. Ethically, it is not an ideal situation. However, it has clearly led to the massive success of the Trump business empire.

OTHER BUSINESS VENTURES

Chapter 6

Due to the major success of Trump's global luxurious real estate business, Trump has been able to expand into various other ventures as well. These ventures have all been more of a hobby opportunity, and are mostly funded by the money he earned through his real estate company. There is an incredibly long list of endeavors that Trump has embarked on, so we have only included the most memorable ones here. Trump has done everything from launch his own board game to his own personal steak brand. He even owned a sports team at one time and had a major short-term impact on the football league he was involved in. Trump's many ventures have mostly ended in failure or with failure to continue thriving, though some have wound up to be excellent additions to his company's income. Below is a list of Trump's many business attempts, including some of his best successes, and some of his most memorable failures.

Golf Courses

Donald Trump and his company, The Trump Organization, currently operate 17 different golf courses and resorts. These resorts are located in various areas of the world, with a few in the United States. He makes approximately $382 million worth of revenue per year from these golf courses and resorts, as of the year 2015. These golf courses are some of the most luxurious, and most famous golf courses across the world. With stunning views, spectacular courses, and luxurious green grass, these have definitely turned up to be one of

Trump's more successful ventures. Trump even boasts about his golf courses on his personal website, where he showcases each of the 17 courses and resorts, complete with their individual stats and websites.

Sports Involvement

Aside from his very successful golf venture, Trump has had some involvement in other areas of the sporting world. At one time, Trump owned the New Jersey Football Team, "The Generals." Around the same time, in 1983, the United States Football League (USFL) formed, and Trump's team became a charter member. The league played its first three seasons during the spring and summer. After some negotiations and convincing, Trump encouraged the majority of the team owners of other USFL teams to have the USFL moved to the fall in 1986. This meant the league would play opposite of the National Football League (NFL). Trump argued that this transition would force a merge to take place between the two leagues, meaning that it would increase their investment. Instead, it led to continuing financial troubles which eventually forced the USFL to fold.

At one time, Trump was involved in a cycling race. The purpose was to try and create a race Equivalent to "Tour de France" for America. Trump called the race *Tour de Trump*. However, two years after its run, Trump withdrew his sponsorship due to financial troubles among his other business ventures. The race was renamed *Tour DuPont* and continued to be held for several years after.

In 2014, Trump was reported to have made an unsuccessful attempt at purchasing the NFL's team "Buffalo Bills."

Beauty Pageants

From the years 1996-2015, Trump was the owner of the majority of three major beauty pageants: "Miss Universe" as well as "Miss USA" and its younger counterpart "Miss Teen USA." Originally, the three pageants aired on CBS. Trump, however, was dissatisfied with the scheduling of his pageants, so he moved two of them to NBC. The official move of the Miss Universe and Miss USA pageants took place in the year 2002.

The airing of Trump's pageants on NBC and NBCUnivision ended following a controversial presidential campaign remark made in 2015. Trump was recorded making remarks about illegal Mexican immigrants. The termination of their business relationship led Trump filing a $500 million lawsuit against the network, claiming they were breaching their contract, as well as for defamation.

In September 2015, Trump claimed he "settled" the lawsuits by declaring his sole ownership over the Miss Universe Organization. He purchased NBC's share in the organization and closed his lawsuits against the network. Shortly after, he sold his own shares of the Miss Universe Organization to WME/IMG.

Trump Model Management

Trump founded a modeling company in 1999, called "Trump Model Management." He operates the company SoHo, Manhattan, New York. Trump has a secondary company called Trump Management Group LLC, and together, both of his companies have been responsible for introducing nearly 250 foreign fashion to the United States since the year 2000. In the year 2014, Alexia Palmer, a former model of the Trump agencies, sued the Trump Model Management company as well as the president of the company, Corrine Nicolas, and other company managers. The lawsuit was based on alleged racketeering, mail fraud, breach of contract, and violation of immigrant wage laws. In March 2016, the U.S Federal Court dismissed the case.

Trump University

Trump opened his own for-profit company geared towards education. Trump University was a company which ran various real estate trainings and other programs. The company operated from 2005 until it closed its doors sometime around 2010. The University has since closed, following several lawsuits being filed against it.

Trump University was founded in 2005 by Donald Trump and his associates Jonathan Spitalny and Michael Sexton. The university was known for offering training courses that specifically covered the topics of asset management, real estate, entrepreneurship, and wealth creation. The courses were priced from anywhere between $1,500 and $35,000.

In 2005, Trump University was reported for misuse of the word "university," with the report claiming its use violated the state law. In 2010, a second notification was received. Following the second notification, the trio changed the name of the operation to "Trump Entrepreneurial Institute." In addition to the notification, the state held Trump personally liable for his failure to acquire a business license in order to run the operation.

Shortly before it closed its doors, a $40 million civil lawsuit was filed against the Institute by the state of New York in 2013. The lawsuit claimed that Trump University was making false claims and defrauding their consumers. On top of the state's civil lawsuit, there were two additional class-action civil lawsuits filed in federal court. In these cases, Donald Trump and his company were personally named. The purpose and outcome of these cases remain unknown.

Donald J. Trump Foundation

This private foundation is based in the U.S and was founded in 1988. The foundation's initial purpose was to donate proceeds from Trump's first book: *Trump: The Art of the Deal*. Despite its original purpose, Trump hardly ever donated any money, and instead, the foundation's funding was mostly acquired through various donors. The top donors from 2004 to 2014 were Trump's friends, Vince and Linda McMahon. The couple is from World Wrestling Entertainment and was responsible for a total of $5 million worth of donations made to the Donald J. Trump Foundation following Trump's 2007 appearance on the show WrestleMania.

Based on the foundation's tax return, the Donald J. Trump Foundation had donated some money to various health care charities, as well as some sports-related charities and some conservative groups. In 2016, however, *The Washington Post* began reporting on the foundation, revealing that the foundation was potentially responsible for several legal and ethical violations. The violations that were reported include: potential tax-evasion and self-dealing. In October 2016, the Foundation has issued a notice to immediately cease its fundraising activities in New York, by the New York Attorney General's office.

Branding and Licensing

Due to the popularity of Trump's brand, he has included his name as a part of a branding and licensing venture. Many business developers have been known to pay Trump to market their properties. In turn for their payments, Trump allows them to use his name, and he operates as the public face for their various projects. Due to the nature of this venture, Trump is not the owner of some buildings that display his name. This venture has been one of his most valuable ventures, and has roughly a $562 million evaluation, with a total of 33 licensing projects that are under development. 7 of the 33 projects are comprised of Trump International Hotel and Tower "condominium hotels." You can read more about the topic of Trump's brand and how it has contributed to his empire's success in chapter 8.

Trump Airlines

Trump Airlines ran its course from 1989-1992. The official name of the company was Trump Shuttle, Inc. Trump acquired finances from a collection 22 separate banks and used the combined $380 million worth of financing to begin his airline venture. June 23, 1989, was the first day the airline began its service, with its airport hub being located at LaGuardia Airport located in New York City. The airline's flights were scheduled between LaGuardia and Logan Airport in Boston, in addition to the Washington National Airport (now the Ronald Reagan Airport) located in Washington, D.C and the Orlando Airport in Florida.

Almost immediately, the airline began having problems. Ultimately, the airline never turned a profit. In September 1990, just shy of a year and a half of its operations, the airline's loans went into default. While the airline offered unusual luxuries, such as laptop rentals, it failed to serve the needs of the clientele. In addition to failed ability to meet clientele needs, there was a massive increase in the price of jet fuel at the time, as a result of the first war in Iraq. Essentially, the combination of the two resulted in the failure of Trump Shuttle, Inc.

In April 1992, the airline officially ceased its operations and was merged into its successor: Shuttle, Inc., which was later renamed to US Air Shuttle. The only remnant of the failed airline venture is Trump's personal aircraft: a 43-seat customized Boeing 757. The plane is outfitted with all of the luxuries required to fly "Trump Style" and is Trump's source of transportation from place to place.

Trump Vodka

Produced by The Trump Organization, Trump Vodka was an American vodka brand. The vodka was launched in the United States in 2005. Within' 6 years of its launch, the vodka failed to meet the required threshold distribution. In 2011, the sales of Trump Vodka in the United States of America ceased. Despite its failure in America, however, the vodka continues to be sold in Israel, where its popularity increases around Passover (a Jewish Holiday.)

Drinks America, the partner who signed with Donald Trump to promote the vodka brand, was subjected to several lawsuits surrounding the vodka brand during its sales window. For example, Bruni Glass sued the company over some unpaid bills. This lawsuit led to an altercation between Bruni Glass and Trump's vodka company, which ultimately resulted in 500,000 mini bottles of Trump Vodka being melted in a furnace instead of being shipped to the company. Even Trump himself sued Drinks America over unpaid royalties. However, due to the case being taken up at the wrong level of court, it was dismissed from a "lack of subject matter jurisdiction."

Trump: The Game

Trump: The Game was a board game that was initially launched in 1989 by the Milton Bradley Company. Trump stated that a percentage of the revenue would be donated to charities that benefited cerebral palsy, as well as AIDS research, though the percentage remained undisclosed. Due to poor sales, though, the game was no longer produced or sold. At the time, the game was expected to sell 2 million copies but wound up selling around 800,000. However, following Trump's successful appearances on the NBC reality TV series "The Apprentice," Parker Brothers decided to re-launch the game in 2004.

The game was made to resemble Monopoly and featured many of the same pieces and rules. The 1989 version was slightly different from the 2004 version in that there were fewer "Trump Cards" fewer "property boxes" and an additional dice. The number of players (4) remained the same, as well as the currency.

Despite its fleeting success during 2004, the game was deemed a failure as it was inferior to the already-famous and well-loved game of Monopoly. *Time Magazine* featured an article in 2011 with the game listed in "Top 10 Donald Trump Failures," with the game being referred to as one of Trump's "ridiculous ideas." Two additional print articles featured it as one of Trump's business failures.

Trump Magazine

Featuring mostly comics and short stories, Trump Magazine only featured two issues. The first issue made its appearance in January 1957. The magazine was published by Playboy Mansions' own Hugh Hefner and was edited by the well-known cartoonist and editor Harvey Kurtzman. The magazine featured a mascot which was a trumpeter herald stylized after the Alice in Wonderland illustrations by John Tenniel.

It was reported that Trump Magazine boasted great sales, especially considering it was a new magazine that featured a 50-cent cover price. At the time, a 50 cent price tag was considered a significantly high price for magazines. Unfortunately, the cost of production was higher than its profitable value and the magazine failed to produce more than 2 issues.

Trump Steaks

Launched in 2007, Trump Steaks is, as you may have guessed, a steak brand. Initially, the steaks were sold at The Sharper Image and QVC. The steaks were incredibly pricey, ranging from $199-$999 for a 4-pack. You could only order the steaks through the catalog, which was featured in the Sharper Image magazine. The steaks sales were discontinued after a short two-month run due to the sales being incredibly poor and the overall venture being deemed unsuccessful. In December 2014, the Trump Steak trademark was canceled. As of 2016, the steaks are no longer available for purchase in The Sharper Image stores. However, they can still be purchased through a number of Trump's properties.

Trump Mortgage

Another one of Trump's failed business ventures, Trump Mortgage failed after housing sales, and sale prices dropped in the 2008 recession. The company was launched in 2006, and Trump claimed his belief was that housing sales would remain strong for a long time to come. Despite the fall of the company, Trump refused to take any responsibility for it, stating he had not been involved in the management of the company and that the executives in charge failed to perform properly.

Trump Merchandise

On Trump's own website, he has a featured section called "Merchandise – Donald J. Trump Collection." The page features a selection of suits, ties, accessories, wallets, and eyewear he has personally designed. In addition to his fashion line, he has a fragrance line, a home décor line, and several books he has co-written.

Max Vanguard

Chapter 7

One of Trump's more successful business ventures includes his extensive involvement in film and television. Over his lifetime, Trump has been no stranger to the world of film. In fact, when he built his first-ever Trump Tower in New York, he included a special studio dedicated specifically to filming. Over his many years in business, Trump has been involved in several different television series, documentaries, talk shows, and other filmed events. While this filming venture has been somewhat of a fun hobby for the famous businessman, it has also offered an incredible marketing opportunity for his business. Featuring on television in the way he has, particularly with his popular run on The Apprentice, enabled him to get his name, brand, and company on national television. This type of successful branding and marketing has encouraged the success of his business and the popularity of his brand by getting his name out there and encouraging people to become more interested in his business and many additional side ventures he embarked on.

Producer

Trump has been a credited producer 19 times according to his IMDB profile. Of those credits includes various Miss Universe and Miss USA Pageants, The Apprentice, a TV series documentary about his business, and as an executive producer on The Girls of Hedsor Hall. For some of the productions, such as the Miss Universe and Miss USA pageants, Trump was the primary investor and sponsor for the televised events. For others, he was involved for various other reasons, potentially including his lengthy experience with The Apprentice, his networking connections, and other reasons that would benefit the TV shows.

Actor

In addition to being a producer, Trump has been a credited actor in 20 different films and television series'. In many of these credits, he appeared as a cameo under his own name, which is where the brilliant marketing opportunity comes into play. Trump can be seen in various films as acting as himself. He has also starred as the actor who played Waldo's Dad in The Little Rascals, as a VIP Patron in 54, as Daniel Ray McLeech in Sabrina, The Teenage Witch, and as an extra on both Monk, and Horrorween.

WWE and WrestleMania

Trump is a friend of World Wrestling Entertainment (WWE) owner Vincent McMahon, as well as a major WWE fan himself. In the Trump Plaza, Trump has been the host for two WrestleMania events and has actively participated in numerous WrestleMania shows. In fact, in 1991, Trump's hosted the WBF Championship at the Trump Taj Mahal casino in Atlantic City. This championship was owned by WWF. (In 1991, the WWE was called the "World Wrestling Federation" or the WWF.)

At WrestleMania 23, there was a match titled "The Battle of the Billionaires," in which Trump appeared. On this episode, Trump and Vince McMahon were in opposing corners with two famous wrestlers fighting for them. Bobby Lashley fought for Trump's corner, and Umaga fought for McMahon's corner. Stone Cold Steve Austin featured as the event's special guest referee. The match operated on the circumstance that the loser's corner would have the billionaire shave their head. Vincent McMahon wound up having his hair shaved, as Lashley was the winner.

In 2013, the McMahon's and WWE inducted Trump into the celebrity wing of the WWE Hall of Fame. The induction took place at the Madison Square Garden in New York and was based on his contributions to promoting the organization. The next night, Trump made his sixth WrestleMania appearance.

The Apprentice

The Apprentice was one of the first opportunities for many people to get a real insight to Trump. This was an opportunity for the businessman to step further into the limelight and be regarded by many for his success and fortune. In the year 2003, Trump became the host and executive producer of the reality show. The show was held in Trump's New York-based Trump Tower in its very own film television studio set.

The Apprentice was a reality show that featured a variety of individuals who competed for high-level management jobs within' one of Trump's various commercial enterprises. The contestants of the show were eliminated one by one from the challenge throughout the 14 episodes of each season of the show until one remained and was announced the winner. The show led Trump trademarking his popular catchphrase from the show: "You're fired."

The first year of The Apprentice Trump earned $50,000 per episode or a total of about $700,000 for the entire season. However, following the major success of the show, Trump received an enormous pay increase. The following season it is believed that Trump earned roughly $1 million per episode or about $14 million per season.

Due to his hosting of the reality show, in 2007 Trump received his own star on the Hollywood Walk of Fame. However, in his presidential campaign of 2016, the star was targeted for vandalism.

Following his time hosting The Apprentice, Trump was hired to host The Celebrity Apprentice alongside producer Mark Burnett. The Celebrity Apprentice was a spin-off of The Apprentice and was a show where major celebrities would compete in order to win money for their respective charities. Though the show was co-produced by Trump and Burnett, Trump was the one who remained in the forefront and was responsible for deciding who would win and who would be "fired" or eliminated from the show. There were several succeeding international variations of The Apprentice franchise that were also co-produced by Trump and Burnett.

NBC announced their renewal for The Apprentice's 15th season on February 16, 2015. However, Trump denied the position for hosting the season as he was facing the possibility of running in the presidential election. Despite his decision not to return as a host, NBC announced that they were going to continue with production anyway. After his controversial presidential campaign and the widespread negative reaction from the public for his derogatory statements regarding immigrants, on June 29, 2016, NBCUniversal issued a statement claiming that they were terminating their business relationship with Trump.

Other Filmography

In addition to his above features, Donald Trump has been seen across TV and film many other times. He has been credited as appearing as himself over 230 times on television, including several documentaries and TV specials regarding his most recent presidential campaign. In addition to his appearances alongside his opponent Hillary Clinton, he has appeared in over 25 other television series, including various talk shows and comedy series. Some of the most recognizable shows he's been featured on include: The Arsenio Hall Show, WWE specials, CMT Music Awards, The Passionate Eye, The Jay Leno Show, Rachel Ray, David Letterman, Jimmy Kimmel, and more.

Awards

On top of all of the above, Trump has also been involved in soundtracks, special thank-you videos, and in various archive footages at historical events. As you can see, Trump is no stranger to the world of television. For all of his involvement, he has been subjected to awards ceremonies and an induction into the WWE Celebrity Wing Hall of Fame. He also won a Razzie Award and his own Star that was placed on The Hollywood Walk of Fame. He has been nominated six times for a combination of other awards, including the Primetime Emmy Award twice, an OFTA Television Award, a second Razzie Award, and the Teen Choice Award. So, not only has he been featured on television and in various films over 300 times, he has also been awarded for his features. All of this success in the world of film has only increased his success, contributed to his recognition and popularity, and likely driven him to further success in his business empire.

BOOKS AND PRINT

Chapter 8

As with many major business individuals, Trump has come out with a series of books focused on helping people increase their knowledge in business, investments, and other areas he has been involved in. Many of his books have been a major success, and have also contributed as their very own pillar in his empire.

In total, Trump has co-written 20 books. Of the books, there are titles attributed to the topic of the United States of America and its status, business tips and strategies, and a book about golf. The first book he ever released was in 1987 and was co-written with author Tony Schwartz. The book is still in print today and can be purchased from any number of bookstores, or rented from the library. This book is titled "The Art of the Deal" and offers a significant amount of business advice, with the emphasis on assisting fellow businessmen and women alike to make successful business deals. There is a variety of useful information between the book's covers, including topics such as, but not limited to: protecting your assets, knowing your market, getting the word out, and having fun. This book also features a German title, which boasts all of the same information and value, only in German. It is one of five books that has a translated copy for a different language.

In addition to his initial book, Trump has launched several other books with the purpose of assisting people in enhancing their business strategies and increasing their success in the business world. The majority of his books, in fact, are based on business and increasing your wealth, with a total of 14 titles in addition to his first book launch "The Art of the

Deal." Those twelve titles include 10 that are attributed to business strategies and 4 that are focused on increasing your wealth. These titles include:

- Surviving at the Top (released in 1990)
- The Art of Survival (released in 1991)
- The Art of the Comeback (co-written with Kate Bohner, released in 1997)
- The Way to the Top: The Best Business Advice I Ever Received (released in 2004)
- How to Get Rich (released in 2004)
- Think Like a Billionaire: Everything You Need to Know About Success, Real Estate, and Life (released in 2004)
- How to Build a Fortune: Your Plan for Success From the World's Most Famous Businessman (released in 2006)
- Why We Want You to be Rich: Two Men – One Message (co-written with Robert Kiyosaki, released in 2007)
- Think Big and Kick Ass in Business and Life (co-written with Bill Zanker, released in 2007)
- The Best Real Estate Advice I ever Received: 100 Top Experts Share Their Strategies (released in 2007)
- Trump 101: The Way to Success (released in 2007)
- Never Give Up: How I Turned My Biggest Challenges into Success (released in 2008)

- Think Like a Champion: An Informal Education in Business and Life (released in 2009)
- Midas Touch: Why Some Entrepreneurs Get Rich – and Why Most Don't (co-written with Robert Kiyosaki, released in 2011)

While most of his titles have been with the purpose of giving knowledge in business and wealth, there have also been a few that have been based on the status of the United States, as well as one on golf. One of these titles: The America We Deserve (written with Dave Shiflett and released in 2000) was launched at the time of his first presidential campaign that ran for a brief time from 1999-2000 before he withdrew himself from the race. The book was used as leverage to increase his following, promote his position on the important elements of American politics, and help him with greater success in the likelihood of winning the election. He also launched two additional books around the same time as his presidential campaign for 2015-16, which was likely done for the same reason as he did in 2000. These books were based on the problems America faces in modern times, and Trump's opinion on how they should be rectified. The titles he wrote about America, and the one about golf includes:

- The America We Deserve (written with Dave Shiflett, released in 2000)
- The Best Golf Advice I Ever Received (released in 2005)

- Time to Get Tough: Making America No. 1 Again (released in 2011)
- Crippled America: How to Make America Great Again (released in 2015)
- Great Again: How to Fix Our Crippled America (released in 2016)

In addition to his 20 book titles, Trump has been involved in writing he has also had 24 books written about him and his businesses. Trump has also been featured in hundreds of magazine articles, newspaper articles, internet posts, and more. Of the articles he's been involved in, he was either the topic of the article or involved in an interview format. His involvement in various nationally recognized publications only grew with his presidential campaign and presidential victory and will continue to grow as he rules as President of the United States from 2016-2020.

Max Vanguard

Chapter 9

Aside from his multi-billion-dollar real estate business, there has been one other major pillar in the success of Trump's business empire. With thanks to his many endeavors, the entire Trump Brand has been an important part of the creation of Trump's success. While he specializes in real estate and golf courses and resorts, he has also tried his hand with many other endeavors, as we previously discovered. While not every attempt was successful, he has still managed to get his name in front of the masses several times over the past 50 years. While each of his endeavors has created the pillars of his empire, it can be argued that Trump's business empire is largely based on the popularity of the Trump Brand. Even though the brand was started by his predecessors, and then he was introduced to the brand by his father, it can be argued that Donald was responsible for turning the family's brand into what it is today. After all, it was Donald Trump who turned the small New York-based real estate business into a multi-billion-dollar, global organization responsible for some of the most well-known pieces of real estate across the world.

The Trump brand was founded by Donald's paternal grandmother: Elizabeth Trump. The family business was formerly known as Elizabeth Trump & Son, but under Donald's ownership, the name was changed to The Trump Organization. This organization is responsible for overseeing all of the Trump-related business endeavors, including real estate investments, business ventures, and Trump-branded products (including the steaks and vodka.) The company was originally operated by Donald's grandfather, but following his death moved to the ownership of his grandmother and his father, as they maintained the family real estate business following his grandfather's passing. It was said that Elizabeth Trump had an incredible talent at maintaining the business following her husband's passing, and was able to maintain the family's income. As her son, Frederick Trump grew older, he assisted in maintaining the family business. It was Frederick who gave Donald his first opportunity in the real estate industry through the family's business, while Donald was still in school for real estate studies. Like his father gave him his winning opportunity in the business world, Donald opted to provide the same opportunity to his own children.

The Trump brand is headed by The Trump Organization, which all three of Trump's eldest children work for. Prior to his presidential victory, Trump also played a major role in the business. However, his victory leads to his involvement in his business being a conflict of interest, and therefore he has passed all of the responsibility down to his children, at least for the duration of his presidential reign. His eldest children have all been involved in the brand since their earlier years. Donald Jr. and Ivanka joined the family business just a year after their college graduations, and Eric joined the business immediately following his college graduation. Due to their extensive work with the company, they are fully familiar with the operations of the business and are believed to be able to fully manage the company without the assistance of their father, at least for the next four years.

The brand has been grown organically through the years by purchasing major successful (and failed) real estate holdings and, in many instances, turning them for profit. He has also purchased and operated businesses under the family name, as well as started many product launches under the family name. Some of these launches include Trump: The Game, Trump Steaks, Trump Vodka, and Trump Magazine. Although many of the endeavors never panned out, they all gave Trump the opportunity to put his business in the spotlight, even if only for fifteen minutes of fame. Many times, the endeavors returned more embarrassing reports than anything else, but regardless, their name was still out there. Perhaps it is in part due to the consistent exposure that has contributed to the brand being nationally-recognized.

The Trump name has become so famous in America, as well as across the world, that many projects have actually requested that the Trump name be used, despite Trump not actually being involved. This growth in branding has assisted in further marketing the family name, while also returning the successful businessman with a nice profit. He gets paid to promote the project, as well as have his name used in the project title. Due to this, there are actually several businesses out there that boast the Trump name but aren't actually owned by the Trump's.

At this time, The Trump Organization maintains its highest level of success through real estate. The organization is responsible for many investments, as well as for purchasing and selling luxurious real estate holdings. With the entire family in on the deal, it has helped increase the name popularity by increasing its "family focus." Now, Ivanka Trump is responsible for overseeing the acquisition of new developments, Eric Trump is responsible for overseeing the building of the developments, and Donald Jr. maintains a position as executive vice president of the company. This has freed up Donald Sr. to be able to pursue his American presidency while giving the children an opportunity to truly learn the responsibilities of the family company. Unfortunately, his unpopular presidential campaign has also damaged his brand's reputation, with many Americans boycotting the brand entirely.

PRESIDENTIAL CAMPAIGN

Chapter 10

In 2015, Trump announced he was going to be entering in the presidential election campaign for the second time. His initial attempt was in 2000, but the brief run in the electoral campaign lasted less than a year before he withdrew himself from the race. However, in 2016 he was victorious in his campaign and was awarded the 2017-2021 presidency. This campaign is what has driven to Trump's most recent rise in popularity, with a heavy mixture of passionate followers, as well as a passionate opposition. For nearly two years, Trump was plastered across mainstream social media, as well as news outlets and magazine articles. He used his knowledge in business and negotiations to argue a radical position and it ultimately ended in his victory for the election.

The 1999-2000 Presidential Campaign

On October 24, 1999, Trump made an appearance on the show "Meet the Press." During that appearance, he made an official announcement stating that he was going to be joining the Reform Party. At one point in the interview, he stated he was better suited for the presidency than a politician because "I understand this stuff." He claimed the Republican Party was going crazy, and the nominee at the time, Buchanan, was a racist. On the first of January in 2000, Trump launched his book "The America We Deserve." The book was promoted during a press conference in the Trump Tower on January 5th. The press conference was aired on a national radio station, C-SPAN. At the conference, Trump signed books and answered reporter's questions, at one point announcing that "I may be too honest to be a politician."

Several conflicts took place within' the Reform Party, between Trump and other members. Disputes occurred over things such as where to hold a convention, how Trump was arguing his position and more. On January 31, 2000, Trump's failure to obtain 5,000 signatures from registered Reform Party members for the New York primary ballot led to his name being removed. Trump continued to attempt to clear the air between himself and the Reform Party but failed to do so. His campaign ended on February 14th, when he declared his official withdrawal from the race. He claimed his reasoning for withdrawal was that the Reform Party was not, he quoted "conductive to victory," and that he "could not win the election running as the party's nominee," and so he decided to discontinue his campaign efforts. At the same time, he expressed his concerns about the party's direction and purpose, and particularly its membership.

The 2015-2016 Presidential Campaign and Victory

15 years following his brief presidential campaign efforts in 2000, Trump announced he was going to run for office once again. On June 16, 2015, Trump officially launched his new presidential campaign. This time, he was serving as the Republican

nominee, following his victory for most votes during the Republican National Convention of 2016. For this election, Trump selected Mike Pence, an Indiana governor, as his vice presidential running mate. After less than a year and a half of campaigning, Trump and Pence were elected for the president and vice president positions of the United States of America on November 8, 2016.

This election has been a major controversy, leading to several post-election riots and protests. Many American citizens have been seeking a recount of votes and demanding that there be a different president in place. This is because, throughout his campaign efforts, Trump made several derogatory, racist, sexist and perverted comments. His commentary throughout the campaign led to severe backlash for him, as he lost a significant amount of support for his businesses and with his existing business relationships. For example, his questionable remarks about illegal Mexican immigrants led to NBCUniversal terminating their business relationship with him and refusing to carry on with any future business endeavors that involved Trump.

His 2015-16 campaign was highlighted by his popular slogan "Make America Great Again!" which was printed on various paraphernalia and sported by Trump and his supporters at many of his speeches, interviews, and debates. Trump held various extreme arguments and positions, one of which included Trump wanting to have a wall built along the entire border between the United States and Mexico, with the belief that it would eliminate the influx of illegal Mexican immigrants into the

United States. He also claimed he wanted to deport immigrants back to their own countries while America renegotiates the terms of its immigration laws, and more. Nearly all of his speeches and conferences included some level of violence as Trump-supporters defended him against peaceful protestors, and he egged them on. He clearly expressed a lack of concern for individuals in the country when he mocked the disabled, berated veterans, had a Mother and her crying baby removed from one of his conferences, made perverted remarks about women, expressed various racist remarks, and much more. This considerably ignorant stance is what led to people having a severe distaste for Trump, and has led to post-election riots and protests, where involved members have adopted the slogan "Not My President!"

Despite the large outcry against him, there is still a significant number of Americans who supported his views and spent their votes on him. On the election night of November 8, 2016, Trump, despite predictions, won in more states than his opponent Hillary Clinton. As a result, the media declared his victory on November 9, 2016, announcing that Trump would begin his four-year presidential reign in January of 2017.

Max Vanguard

WHAT'S IN STORE

Chapter 11

After all of the history between Trump and his family business, it was shocking to watch his presidential campaign potentially sabotage a great deal of his success. Now, due to his new position as president-elect, he is no longer able to oversee his business operations as that would be a conflict of interest and could compromise his presidency. Therefore, he has relinquished the responsibilities to his children and has decided to forego in his presidential reign. With all of the changes in his life, especially ones with such profound effects on his business, it is natural to wonder what is going to happen to his business empire, as well as with Donald Trump himself. Let's take a look at what is projected for Trump's future, and the future of his family business.

Business Life

As required by law, and as we have previously discussed, Trump has stepped down from the chairmanship of The Trump Organization to pursue his presidency over the United States of America. At one time, he claimed that he didn't care about the future of his company, as he was more interested in applying his knowledge to building back the "greatness" of America. He wanted to increase the countries riches, and improve the overall quality of the American economy. Instead of being responsible for his company, which he referred to as "peanuts" in compared to his presidential duties, he would pass the rights and responsibility of the company down to his three eldest children.

While his election has led to major controversy over his brand, as well as several boycotts, it has been reported that this has supposedly had no negative impact on his business. In fact, employees of his companies report that *more* people have visited the Trump Tower than ever before, despite there being ongoing protestors in front of the building. Many believe that Trump's presidency will actually improve the recognition of the brand across the globe, and in turn increase the popularity of the family's brand and further drive it to success. The truth is, regardless of what people may think of him, Trump is an incredibly successful man. In the eyes of business, he has taken his family company and made it incredibly successful – and wealthy – he has involved his family and assisted them in creating their own success while contributing to the family's success, and he has even held personal successes with his presidential victory. This means that, in the eyes of business people across the globe, Trump is a successful man and his company would likely be a very promising business partnership, potentially meaning that even more businesses and people will want to enter business relationships with The Trump Organization and use his brand name to promote their projects.

Family Life

As he takes on his new, demanding role of president of the United States, it is obvious that there will be some shifts in the family functions. With new responsibility being put on the shoulders of his eldest children, and less involvement in his family company, there is a good chance that it will take a while for the shift to become successful. His children will need to learn to take over all of the responsibilities without their father's help, although there is no certainty that Trump will remain *completely* withdrawn from the family company, and Trump will have to shift his focus to the entirety of the country. Therefore, there will be a period of adjustment while everyone gets used to their new roles. His family life at home will likely remain the same, as Melania and he works together to raise their child, Barron Trump. However, many tabloids are eagerly watching their marriage and waiting to see if anything shifts as a result of Trump's presidential campaign. Many speculate that his perverted and derogatory remarks could drive Melania away, but she insists that she maintains her solidarity with her husband and supports him entirely in his new venture.

Presidential Outlook

On the Trump-Pence presidential campaign website, there is a "positions" section that outlines what Trump and Pence plan on doing during their presidential reign. On that section, there are various positions that we heard throughout his presidential campaign, but to recap, we will go over them again here:

- Have a wall erected along the border of Mexico and the United States

- o Trump wants to have a wall built between the two countries to reduce illegal immigrants. He also intends "...to compel Mexico to pay for the wall" as quoted on his presidential website.

- Healthcare Reform
  - o Trump intends to eliminate the existing Obamacare American Affordable Care Act and replace it with an alternative healthcare system.

While those are the only two positions discussed on his presidential campaign website, there have been many more discussed by him through the presidential debates and his various speeches across the nation. Trump has extensive plans to change the immigration laws in America to make them stricter while eliminating all immigrants that could be a potential terrorist risk to the country. He also intends to alter the income tax system, reducing it from 7 tax brackets to 3, as well as enforce other strategies (such as trade protectionism and additional spending on defense and infrastructure) to help grow the American economy. Trump also intends to assist in eliminating the pressures from student debts, and national debts, while restructuring the budget to allow for improvement in areas he deems important, such as the military. He has expressed various other intentions to improve the American economy, as well as the overall country itself, but in many of his arguments, he failed to give detailed information on how he will do so.

At least half of all Americans are dissatisfied with their new president, but there is still a large number of citizens who believe Trump has what it takes to improve America. The outcome is obviously unpredictable, as we have yet to see what he does with America, but based on his presidential campaign, we can conclude that he has big plans too, as he says, "Make America Great Again."

Despite all of his strong claims and profound remarks through his campaign, Trump has already given a good idea as to what type of presidency he will lead. After less than a month of being awarded the presidential victory, Trump has already back-pedaled on several of the claims he clung to during his race. Here are five instances where Trump has already altered his stance and potentially changed his mind on some of his most prominent arguments:

- Obamacare: Trump promised to appeal Obamacare entirely, starting the first day he got into office. However, he has been recorded during a meeting with Obama, stating that he is looking at alternatives to a total repeal, and may consider keeping preexisting conditions.

- A Wall along the border of the Mexico, at the Expense of Mexicans: one of Trump's first and most prominent arguments was to have a wall erected along the border of the United States and Mexico. This is one of the only two positions viewed on his presidential campaigns. Despite his major argument *for* the wall during his campaign, Trump's secretary of state has already been reported with admitting to the argument being a campaign device and said that Trump has admitted that he may not spend much time getting Mexico to pay for the wall.

- Terminate the "War On Coal": Trump argued that coal is, quote, "...an abundant, clean, affordable, reliable domestic energy resource. Those who mine it and their families should be protected from the Democratic Party's radical anti-coal agenda." This argument led to many being fearful of the fate of global warming under the Trump presidency. However, Trump doesn't intend to do much with the coal industry, other than just leave it the way it is.

- Mass Deportations to Eliminate Illegal Immigrants: this was one of Trump's most well-known, and controversial stances throughout the campaign. He has been quoted saying that he wanted to deport all illegal immigrants, as well as any who were descendants from the countries that have direct conflict with America. He claimed that these individuals were "potential terrorists" and that until America could reinstate new, more effective laws, they needed to leave the country. However, a national radio station hosted an interview where the chairman of the Republican Party claimed that Trump only intended to deport those who had already committed crimes, no one else.

- Removal of Iran Peace Treaty: Trump claimed he would "renegotiate" the peace treaty with Iran, and was quoted to have called it the "stupidest deal of all time." However, there have been reports that Trump does not intend to scrap the treaty at all, and that the renegotiation wouldn't do much to change the current situation.

Despite having a strong, controversial election campaign, Trump has appeared to back-pedal on many of his statements. It appears that he is handling his presidential victory the same as he does with his businesses: by using strategies that allow him to gain control and then using his control to essentially do whatever he wants. It will be interesting to see where the country goes under his presidency, and whether or not he will proceed with any of his radical statements that gained him his victory in the first place.

Max Vanguard

CONCLUSION

Donald J. Trump has been a successful business mogul for nearly his entire life. While he started out with his family in a modest home, and a middle-class real estate business, he quickly built his empire and became one of the most famous businessmen of modern day America. Trump has faced several victories throughout his life, including his success as a real estate investor, the evolution of his family business into a business empire, and his victorious campaign for which he became president of the United States of America.

While the future of Trump's empire and career life remain somewhat of a mystery, one thing is for certain: Trump is likely to lead his future endeavors with the same fierce strategies as he has led all of his previous ventures with. Hopefully, his aggressive and tactical strategies will lead America into the same success that his businesses have experienced, though many Americans do not have faith in his ability to do so. With very little political experience, many fear that Trump's business-oriented tactics will not work in leading their country to victory. Only time will tell if this business mogul will turn out to be a successful president, or if his time in office will turn out to be just another short-lived, unpopular venture for his career.

I want to take the time to thank you for reading *Trump Business: The Business Empire of Donald Trump*. This book was created with the intention of providing insight to the world of Donald J. Trump and his successful business empire. In this book, you have learned all about Trump's upbringing, as well as his education and the foundation for his empire. You have also learned about his family and their contributions to his success, and the various business ventures Trump has embarked on, following the success of his luxurious real estate company.

I sincerely hope that you were able to learn all about Donald Trump and how he successfully built his business empire both through business strategy and the development of his personal life. Throughout all of his ventures and growth, Trump has spent a great deal of his life involved in various business ventures that have ultimately lead to his experience and knowledge in operating a successful business. Regardless of personal opinions on the man, it can't be denied that Trump is an incredibly successful, wealthy and famous businessman. From his business career to his political career, and even among his children and family, Trump has claimed some impressive victories and been responsible for an incredible amount of success. If you enjoyed reading this book and felt that it provided you with the knowledge you were looking for, I ask that you please take the time to rate it on Amazon Kindle. Your honest feedback on *Trump Business: The Business Empire of Donald Trump* would be greatly appreciated.

Finally, thank you for reading this book, I hope you enjoyed it and discovered the value you were seeking.

HILLARY CLINTON: TRUTH AND LIES

Book 3

Max Vanguard

INTRODUCTION

I want to thank you and congratulate you for downloading the book Hillary Clinton: Truth and Lies.

This book contains proven steps and strategies on how to become a truly knowledgeable voter with regard to the Democratic nominee Hillary Clinton. Clinton has been under fire from the beginning of her political career to the present for lying and breaking the rules. Making a decision about whom to vote for in this year's election is a personal thing, yet it can impact us all for at least the next four years.

Here's an inescapable fact: Hillary Clinton has already made history as the first female presidential nominee of any party. Clinton has also earned a negative reputation resulting from scandals and cover-ups in her own personal pursuit of power and money. You need to gain valuable and critical insight into the mindset of this candidate before you decide to vote for her.

If you do not develop your ability to gain critical insight into how Hillary Clinton makes judgments in her thought process and recognize the patterns of her deceit before the fall elections, you may find you voted for the wrong candidate after it's too late. It is your duty as an American citizen to be well-informed.

It's time for you to become an amazing expert in assessing the mental consistencies demonstrated by this fascinating candidate who has over twenty years' experience in key areas of the political framework of this country. History has documented the role of Hillary Clinton in a number of scandals that have cost this country the lives of its citizens, compromised national security, and spent many millions of taxpayer dollars for investigations. Your vote has value; don't give it away without knowing the facts!

TRUTH, LIES AND POLITICS

Chapter 1

The main questions that must be asked are simple. What is the truth? What is a lie? Any child can tell you the difference. Somehow, as we age, we come to believe that when educated, wealthy individuals or people shown in the media tell us something we should automatically believe it as truth. We all know the difference between right and wrong. Once a person lies to you, do you ever trust them again? For years, people have been saying they don't believe half of what they see or hear and for good reason. Everyone has an agenda that they are trying to push. Politicians try and push their policies. Advertisements try and push their products.

Politicians make empty promises all the time; it's the status quo of the business. Are empty promises lies? Most people agree that they are.

Is being in denial the same as lying? This is a different way of looking at the concept, but the answer again is yes. Proving it in an investigation is something different.

When we are talking about running the country, is telling a "white lie" bad? Remember, we're not talking about if you liked grandma's soup or not. Dishonest behavior exhibited by anyone is a red flag and warrants close attention.

Psychology

Facts help your intuition. We've often heard that "if something sounds too good to be true, then it usually is" works well in these cases. Sometimes you just have a feeling but no proof, until one day you notice a fact that substantiates your feeling.
A proven strategy is to approach issues from the common sense side of our brains. By not thinking clearly and making sound decisions it is no wonder we are labeled by foreign countries as being led along unassumingly like sheep.

Salespeople and politicians both use the psychology of the mind to make you buy into what they are selling. They tell you what you want to hear. Political candidates are trying to sell you on electing them, often belittling their opponent in the process.

The Power of the Media

When you turn on the news, you see a person telling you something, and you believe it. How many times have you heard someone say, "I can't believe it's raining? The weatherman said it was supposed to be sunny today." As if it's his fault it rained because he said it would be sunny the day before on television. Watching people in groups lie to each other to get rewarded on reality shows makes the public think this is okay to do in everyday life. This is very powerful stuff.

Lawyers

Being an attorney was considered the most noble profession up until about 75 years ago. Contemporary times say lawyers are liars with a license to steal. Many have a bad reputation and are labeled "ambulance chasers," always looking for other people's money.

People become lawyers to make money. Some practice law while others get into politics. In both cases, you need to have an ego to get to the top. It's a power trip. You need to exaggerate and embellish yourself to stand out and look better than you are, otherwise you become an also-ran.

Why do lawyers get into politics? Many lawyers leave practice to enter politics using the connections they have to form new relationships with businesses and high-ranking individuals, all in the name of money and power.

As a lawyer, Hillary knows the rules and, more importantly, how to break them.

Politicians

Once upon a time, in the early years of the government of this country, politicians had other vocations and being involved in government positions was a side job with no benefits. The corruption began when they became full-time positions with all the "perks."

Politicians usually have a legal background they use as a stepping stone to catapult them into the political arena. Their knowledge of the law makes them ripe for this profession in view of those who elected them. Their familiarity with the law allows them an advantage when discussing bills to be passed.

It's amazing how the current crop of politicians have previous involvement in dirty deeds of the past. It seems to suggest some sort of nepotism/incestuous clan where politicos get recycled. This has been going on for years.

The popular consensus is that they don't serve the people that elected them, they serve themselves.

Elections

The goal in politics is for a candidate to win the election. The powerful money backing the candidates with donations, also known as "big business" of some kind (like big pharma) and special interest groups, put pressure on their candidate to win at all costs and by any means necessary. So what are we as citizens supposed to do? All the static around us in the form of distractions are taking our thinking away from the matters that really count. Are we told the truth from the media, or is it slanted?

Politicians in general have been labeled as liars since pretty much the dawn of government. Not one politician in contemporary times who told the truth and followed through one hundred percent of the time comes to mind. Honor and respect don't exist. It's business as usual. That is how everyone perceives the system.

Dodging questions with a lot of words that say nothing is common—just like any speech from a veteran political figure who is trying to force a cover-up of something they did wrong.

You can't make an omelet without breaking some eggs. Doing damage to your opponent to get what you want is considered appropriate in politics.

Government

Supposedly, we voluntarily elect our government officials in this country. Historically, it is based on choosing a candidate for the government of the people, by the people, and for the people.

It is a fact; history is written by the victors. Before democracy, those with the most power ruled. It was

called "might makes right" when bullies ruled. Then we became civilized and decided to vote for folks to represent us. People who supposedly were very knowledgeable and had the best interests in mind of the people they represented in a party.
Ethics is a big issue; not surprisingly, there is a committee on this. It's to protect the people from the officials they elected and to maintain order where finances are exchanged. This can be seen mostly in banking and insurance.

Mudslinging - Dirty Politics

Even the accusations about Hillary's opponents are lies. Conjuring up stories about your opponents is all part of the game, but Hillary is taking this to a new level in her campaign. At this time, she doesn't have as much mud to sling since she is in a compromised position from the resulting email debacle and her acceptance of Bill's womanizing behavior.

Max Vanguard

HILLARY HISTORY

Chapter 2

Early Years

Born Hillary Rodham, she grew up in Park Ridge, Illinois, in a conservative republican household. A demonstrated achievement-oriented student, she graduated high school in the top five percent of her class. In 1969, she graduated from Wellesley College with a BA in political science along with departmental honors. From there she went on to Yale Law School where she met Bill Clinton. After earning her JD in 1973, she began postgraduate work and, in 1974, served as a member of the impeachment inquiry staff during Watergate.

Political Party

With her father Hugh Rodham being a staunch republican and supporter of Barry Goldwater, Hillary began as a supporter of that party. This would continue until, while in college, she came to dislike how the Nixon campaign portrayed Rockefeller at the Republican National Convention in 1968. She has been a democrat ever since.
Mindset Formatives
We all admire and are influenced by people, mostly as we are growing up but even in adulthood. They help form who we become. It was natural for her to start out as a republican since that was her initial exposure growing up. She shows her independence and ability to form her own opinion in time. It is interesting to note two people who Hillary Clinton

says she admired, Margaret Sanger and Saul Alinsky, and to see now how they influenced her mindset today. Both were outspoken public figures who were involved in thrusting change upon the world, albeit for very different reasons. The basis of the power to move people in certain directions is what Hillary is all about.

Margaret Sanger

Sanger was an early eugenics advocate, feminist, racist, and founder of Planned Parenthood. Her writings reveal the lifelong passion of her beliefs. Hillary has, on more than one occasion, stated she admired Sanger's life and leadership and viewed it as a time that was the most transformational in human history. It is apparent that through the power of political leadership, Hillary wants to make history. She wants to transform society through her political power. An example is her attempt at Healthcare Reform in 1993. Along with that power comes big money, which we have seen is a motivator as well.

Saul Alinsky

Another individual who served to influence Hillary's mindset during her formative years was Saul Alinsky. One must remember the youth of the 1960s and their radical nature.

Alinsky was an author, radical activist, and community organizer. He moved people and genuinely tried to help the poor and minorities organize to be heard, not ignored. His method was one of pushing to new ground gradually in order to make changes.

Hillary wrote a 92-page senior thesis titled "There Is Only the Fight…" on what she learned from him as she admired the veracity of his beliefs which affected her philosophically. She spoke to him, and they corresponded at length where he even offered her a job (that she declined). It was from him that she became excited about fighting for the causes she believed in, but using her own methodology. The thesis was suppressed by the White House when Hillary became First Lady as it did not want to reveal her extremist and radical views to the world—views that she apparently still has today. Also, it is only available on microfilm that needs to be signed out and not on the internet.

It is apparent in the tone of Hillary's public commentary that she has become her own version of the modern-day crusader, saying she wants what's best for the people, but in the background is brandishing her own agenda. She is intelligent and shrewd but has flaws like everyone else. We find her ambition to transform the public in these contemporary times. She wants to change the system from the inside. That has always been her goal as will be seen in later chapters.

Career Path

After Watergate, she married Bill and soon after co-founded Arkansas Advocates for Children and Families. She was appointed the first female chair of the Legal Services Corporation before becoming a partner at the Rose Law Firm, and ultimately, First Lady of Arkansas.

First Lady and Beyond

While Bill Clinton was running for president back in 1992, he made the comment that if he were to become president, the country would be getting "two for one." At the time, it was taken to mean she would be an involved First Lady and that there would be two knowledgeable, politically savvy, and capable individuals who would share in running the country. Today, looking back, we wonder if he meant that voting him into the presidency back then would be a vote for her in the future.

People often used the term "Billary" from 1993 to 2000, referring to Hillary making decisions for Bill and that she was calling the shots from the background to a degree. The reason they have stayed together is that they complement each other so well. It is clear from the first days of Bill's first term that the presidency was a joint venture between them. She was put in charge of projects, but they were not without issue.

The dossier on Hillary's whole life has been about ambition and getting to the top. She only cares about what she wants, not how she gets it or who falls by the wayside. A number of people who were at odds with Hillary Clinton have died under mysterious circumstances. Thank goodness for the internet saving these bits of history that many forgot or did not know happened during the past 38 years while Hillary was involved in politics.

It's scary the way she lies to the public with such apparent ease, but those lies are starting to catch up with her as evidenced by her low ratings as the 2016 election approaches.

Personality

Much of what you will see in this book has to do with Hillary Clinton's aggressive goals to succeed. Her drive shows through on all counts throughout her career. The deaths, although not directly committed by her, resulted from scandals she was part of and possibly masterminded. There are many of them that occurred over time and have seemed to come about at just the right time as to stifle a testimony or cause a distraction from another scandal.

Her scandals are like drunk driving; it's been done 100 times, but you only need to get caught once to be labeled. Those who get caught have usually done it many times. Even those that get caught often become repeat offenders. They can't stop, and she won't stop. Whether she becomes president or not, there will be other fiascos down the road; it's a part of her, it's who and what she is.

Her reactions to being told she lied or broke the rules are childish. She never apologizes, but instead, says she made a mistake. No one should think they are above the law. When reprimanded for wrongdoings she either says she made a mistake or maintains silence in the hope it will go away and just blow over so that she can move on. Others around her get fired for making smaller mistakes.

As any Sherlock Holmes fan knows, the criminal mind has been said to be a very intelligent, devious, cunning, cold-hearted, and calculating one. Criminals always continue until they are apprehended by the authorities, they just don't stop on their own. Their greed keeps them going like an addiction to a drug, and the crimes become more intense to keep getting that high level of satisfaction.

In the end, Hillary will reach a breaking point, and her undoing will be the enormity of all the scandals put together, the weight of which is undeniable.

WATERGATE

Chapter 3

The Democratic National Committee (DNC) headquarters was located at the Watergate office complex in Washington, D.C.

In 1972, there was a break-in at the DNC and five men were arrested. The investigation revealed evidence that the Nixon administration was involved and that President Nixon himself had recorded conversations in his offices and had attempted a cover-up which was leading to his impeachment, but he resigned in disgrace before impeachment proceedings could be finalized.
A short time after Hillary graduated from Yale Law School she was hired as a staff attorney for the House Judiciary Committee investigating the Watergate scandal.

Jerome Zeifman was assigned as Chief Counsel by his boss at the time, Judiciary Committee Chairman Peter Rodino. It was Rodino who was also the boss of Impeachment Inquiry Special Counsel John Doar. It was Doar who directly supervised Hillary's work.

Zeifman claims he kept a diary of events from Watergate. In it, he maintains he would not give Hillary a recommendation claiming she "[lied, was dishonest, and was unethical.]" This stems from Hillary, having followed orders from Rodino through her supervisor Doar, who took files without questioning an assignment to create a brief that addressed whether Nixon had the right to representation by counsel at evidentiary hearings. Obviously, having honor and showing respect for the process to be done correctly were not issues for her.

Hillary was not fired as was frequently mentioned by famous radio talk show host Rush Limbaugh. Zeifman has been interviewed about his recollections working with Hillary and throughout he has critiqued her in a negative manner. In his book Without Honor: The Impeachment of President Nixon and the Crimes of Camelot released in 1998, Zeifman basically states Hillary did not know what she was doing.

After the impeachment inquiry had disbanded, Hillary failed the District of Columbia Bar, but had passed the Arkansas Bar and went to Arkansas to be with her future husband, Bill Clinton.
Subsequent chapters will discuss her involvement in many other investigations, both while in the White House and after.

What can be seen from Hillary's work at Watergate is that it illustrates her cool disregard for the rules early on in her fledgling career just out of law school. There does not seem to be any moral question as to whether she was involved in doing something wrong.

Max Vanguard

<hr>

WHITEWATER

<hr>

Chapter 4

The Whitewater case began in 1994. In actuality, Whitewater came about from another investigation that was being done regarding the collapse of a financial institution by the name of Madison Guaranty Savings and Loan run by James McDougal. In looking for witnesses to the bank's failure, the names of Bill and Hillary Clinton stood out when David Hale testified.

Hale contended Bill pressured him for a $300,000 loan for the Whitewater investment, but did not want to be named in the transaction. It was Hale's second round of testimony that uncovered the Clintons.

From there it just opened up and proceeded to quickly uncover a series of scandals involving the Clintons. Whitewater was Hillary's first noted involvement in a criminal investigation, but it would not be her last.

In short, Whitewater was an Ozark Mountain property investment failure originated in 1978 by the Clintons and their partners in the deal, the McDougals.

The allegation was regarding a fraudulent loan made to Susan McDougal's marketing company to pay off the debts owed by the two couples.
Independent Counsel Kenneth Starr led the investigation. With new twists and turns it took all

of eight years and millions in taxpayer money to sort out the Whitewater probe.

In the end, the Clintons were never prosecuted, but their knowledge and involvement in Whitewater did open the door to other investigations of both Bill and Hillary. The most notable of these will be explored with relevant detail in the subsequent chapters of this book.

The significance of Whitewater is twofold. First, it served to be like a big ball of connected strings, and when unraveled by the investigation showed a slew of other controversies with the Clintons attached to each one in some way. It was like every mistake they made professionally had been connected like a chain.

Second, it documents Hillary Clinton's personal agenda of doing and saying whatever it takes to prosper.

Apparently, copies of 115 pages of "missing" Rose Law Firm billing records were found in the White House in 1996, but the originals are still missing. They reveal how she had repeatedly met with key figures involved in the Whitewater fiasco. It is interesting to see a common theme of documents gone missing that could be used as evidence to bring charges against her. This is the sign of a true lawyer.

PARDONGATE

Chapter 5

Before President Bill Clinton's second term was to officially expire in 2001, he granted 176 presidential pardons, many of which were signed on his last day in office. These pardons drew a firestorm of controversy because of some of the large financial contributions that were made prior to the pardons. Accusations of using his position for personal gain have been nothing new to Bill, but this put a whole new label on the term "corruption."

Hillary Senate Contributions - Cash for Pardons

One such example is Marc Rich, who was convicted of tax evasion. Rich was indicted on 50 counts of fraud, trading with Iran during the U.S. Embassy hostage crisis, racketeering, and evading more than $48 million in income taxes. All combined, these crimes totaled 300 years in prison.

After indicted, Rich fled the country to Switzerland. His actions put him on the FBI's Most Wanted list. His wife's contributions to the Clinton Presidential library and Hillary's 2000 Senate campaign were significant. He remained in Switzerland until President Clinton pardoned him. Apparently, everyone has a price.

There was an alleged scheme made by Hillary's brothers, Hugh and Tony Rodham, who were purportedly taking money in return for promising presidential pardons.

Carlos Vignali was a convicted drug kingpin serving the sixth of his 15-year term when he was pardoned. Reportedly, Hillary's brother Hugh received large sums for being pardoned which was said to be "very important" to Hillary. It is interesting to note the Vignali family is involved in major real estate transaction business in the Los Angeles, California, area.

Almost ironically, Susan McDougal from the Whitewater scandal was pardoned as was Bill's half-brother Robert for drug charges.

The case involving swindler Glenn Braswell, who was sentenced to three years in prison, was another pardon granted by Bill Clinton. Hugh Rodham was paid hundreds of thousands for a pardon granted by Bill on his last day in office.

Max Vanguard

CATTLE FUTURES TRADING

Chapter 6

One of the items uncovered during Whitewater was a controversial futures trading set of transactions made by Hillary. Futures trading is very risky and speculative; you need to know what you are doing. It also has to be clear that you can lose more money than you invest. Hillary's stated objective was to build financial security and a nest egg.

In 1978, around the same time the Whitewater investment took place, Hillary decided to invest $1,000 in cattle futures trading. Even though the minimum investment required was higher, she still managed to open an account. Her friends who knew her at the brokerage made an exception, and she bought on margin. Just ten months later she cashed out, having amassed about $100,000 by mid-1979. She claims to have schooled herself by studying the market, reading everything she could, and talking to people. Although a very intelligent person, futures investing is complex and, like poker, you can learn the rudiments in about an hour, but it takes years to become proficient. She does admit to both making and losing money during this time, but coming out ahead in the end.

The interesting, and suspicious, piece is that she was steered into this by a friend and fellow lawyer, James Blair, who just happened to be employed as outside counsel to Tyson Foods, which was Arkansas's largest employer at that time. Blair had done very well for himself as a futures trader since

1977 and was forever telling friends about his success in that market.

Also of interest is that the broker to Blair and Hillary Clinton was Robert L. "Red" Bone, manager at Refco, who was under investigation at the time for records violations. A recurring theme is how almost all the people Hillary does business with get investigated. Bone was Blair's legal client and had also been a former executive at Tyson Foods.

The main issue is whether her trading success was skill, luck, inside information, or a scandal of leveraging trades by the key players involved. Skilled investors know it is difficult for a novice to make such a rate of return in such a short period of time. Veteran investor analysts agree that her timing was perfect to catch the biggest cattle boom in history. Oddly enough, she never invested in futures again, saying it was nerve-racking and that she no longer had the stomach for it.

The truth is she made a lot of money in a short period of time, even though there are records showing she did lose in some trades. Whether she did so legally and played by the rules could not be proven one way or the other, but it's a very hard sell for most people to believe.

If she lied about her trading success and profited, this was indeed unethical. Nothing could be proven about the mechanics of what transpired, only her involvement.

Since all of this was discovered in 1994, some 15 years had elapsed, which was well past the statute of limitations. Another case of how convenient it was for her.

As a result, officially, there was never any investigation or charges made against Hillary Clinton. It was her money that was at risk and, during the 10-month period in question, she came out ahead.

VINCENT W. FOSTER JR.

Chapter 7

The Whitewater investigation led to many different scandals. As evidence was being uncovered, pressure was growing within the White House to deliver any information it had. Deputy White House Counsel Vince Foster, a close friend and business partner to Hillary, was in charge of finding and providing that information. As he was in the process of doing his duty, something happened that would forever leave a blemish on the Clinton Administration—Vince Foster allegedly committed suicide.

Background

Vince Foster was an early childhood friend of Bill Clinton. They lived across the street from each other, and later Foster was the Deputy White House Counsel at Bill's request during his initial term as president. Before this, Foster was a partner at the Rose Law Firm and was both a colleague and good friend of Hillary and the family.

All those who knew him say he was a good, honest person who enjoyed his successful career practicing law. He was a former military man, an excellent student and athlete, and president of his graduating class—an outstanding human being on all counts, a perfect front man. Then something went wrong.

Suicide

The suicide in 1993 was from an alleged self-inflicted gunshot wound to the mouth. A torn-up resignation note was found in his briefcase that was missing the piece where his signature should have gone. It is not really clear that it was a suicide note. He was said to have allegedly been suffering from clinical depression for which he was taking medication. It was said he was unhappy with his work in politics and Washington in general.

It should also be noted that just before his death Foster was to be called to testify by Kenneth Starr regarding Whitewater.

Even though no fewer than five investigations were done to confirm suicide from a self-inflicted gunshot wound to the mouth as the manner of death, theories of a cover-up persisted through three years of investigation by Kenneth Starr as part of Whitewater. The conspiracy idea was alleged to damage Bill Clinton. The theory is that Foster knew too much about the Clintons, so he had to pay the ultimate price.

Aftermath

It is alleged, on the night of Foster's death, Hillary had sent Maggie Williams (the First Lady's Chief of

Staff), Patsy Thomasson (White House Administration), and Craig Livingston (Director of White House Security) to illegally enter into Foster's office to steal documents even though White House Counsel Bernard Nussbaum barred anyone from going into the office for any reason. The specific documents targeted were any and all those pertaining to Whitewater and Travelgate showing suspicious Clinton involvement, even going so far as to erase memos with Hillary's initials on them.

After Foster's death, $2.73 million was found in a Swiss bank account, with the account number found in his wallet. It is contended he took money on the side for a cover-up. This is hardly likely since Foster was making $300,000 at his Arkansas law firm as a partner. This was a job he actually liked and planned to go back to after his time in the White House. It is believed this was planted as a way to discredit this very credible man. The paper with the account number could have easily been put in his wallet after his death.

Enter Miguel Rodriguez

Miguel Rodriguez was brought in as the lead investigator for the Office of the Independent Counsel investigating the death of Vince Foster.
From the very beginning, the evidence he found in the investigation did not add up. Rodriguez did not

believe Foster's death to be a suicide. Allegedly, Foster was killed, and his murder was made to look like a suicide.

A bullet hole was also found in his neck, but not reported originally. Even after it was found, the evidence went missing and even today only the single shot to the mouth is blamed for his death. Crime scene photos were doctored to look like a suicide. Falsification of records surfaced, and witness intimidation, tampering, and destruction of evidence were all found by Rodriguez. His best attempts to expose the cover-up fell on deaf ears as no one, especially the Clintons, wanted to believe it was anything more than a suicide.

Ultimately, in disgust, he resigned.

The Motive

The motive for him being killed was that he was an honest person who knew too much about the Clintons. Theorists feel that his testimony would be damaging to his friends and the Clintons. The bottom line from what can be deciphered is that they knew each other and they asked him to take the job. Foster had a good work ethic and he was a trusted friend of the Clintons. But Foster hated the job and working for Hillary, who was now saturated with power, bossy, and mean. The ripped-up pieces of the note found in his briefcase show his dismay if it is real. No signature for the note was ever found. There was a missing piece where his signature should have been. That leads us back to whether the note was real.

This shameful and illegal cover-up most assuredly underscores Hillary Clinton's "win at any cost" attitude and does not put her outside the premise of murdering Vince Foster. It would seem that it was coming down to him or them, and he was out.

Vince and Hillary

Questions about a romantic relationship between Hillary and Vince have come up, but most dismiss it only remarking that Vince seemed to fill the role of the "emotional husband" in Hillary's life. From all accounts, they were close friends and business partners.

Hillary's relationships should only be viewed from the establishment of her mental arrangement to get ahead at all costs and feed her desire for power— that is, if she were to be unfaithful in a relationship with a man it wouldn't matter as long as it served her purpose.

It is evident from her beginning with Watergate that she will do whatever she needs to prop herself up and succeed, even if it means sabotaging others. Her goal is to become president where she thinks she will be able to absolve herself from all her wrongdoings with the attitude of "If I'm president, I can't be all that bad." Just like as the presidential candidate she thinks that by getting this far she is in the clear. Be sure and watch those around her to see who will take the fall next as the scapegoat. Democratic National Convention Chair Wasserman Shultz lost her job in the summer of 2016 after it was revealed that the Democratic Party headquarters was hacked and thousands of documents were leaked out including several damaging emails about Hillary.

BILL'S INDISCRETION

Chapter 8

When Hillary was the Senator of New York, she released an autobiography titled Living History, released in 2003. She chose to be interviewed by Barbara Walters in a one-hour televised special program. The big question was regarding her relationship with her husband who had an affair with Monica Lewinsky. Hillary stated that even though she was furious that Bill did this to her and disrespected their family in front of the country, she still thought of him highly and added that after deep thought and counseling, she decided to forgive him and hoped they could grow old together.

The television special served three things: the first was to promote the book, the second showed her forgiving nature, and the third was to open the door and let people know she would consider running for president in 2008.

Hillary spoke to the BBC about how forgiving Bill was the right choice for her and added that when making a decision such as this, one must consider the personal and professional aspects of life. The takeaway message was, in essence, saying that the image of keeping the family unit together was more appealing to voters. The psychology of stressing forgiveness with family worked because her popularity ratings started to increase. This helped her become the U.S. Senator of New York, but more importantly, she became the star of the Clinton power couple.

In fact, she goes on to explain how historical writing, cultures, and religion convey how liberating it feels to forgive someone, possibly more than for the one being forgiven.

Hillary and Bill met in law school when they were at Yale. She quickly recognized the Rhodes Scholar's womanizing ways. Hillary also noted they formed a very compatible couple. She was serious and focused on the tasks at hand teaching him discipline, while he was more eager to socialize and develop relationships. Bill proposed to Hillary following their graduation. Hillary declined.

She loved him, saw his future potential, and decided to disregard his indiscretions that she knew would continue. She realized her long-term future success was linked to his, and that they complemented each other—that together she could achieve the place in life where she wanted to be in this world. Accepting another proposal, they married in 1975.

When the public found out about all the affairs, she forgave him every time despite the embarrassment and it kept his public approval afloat—simply by virtue of her forgiveness of him.

When the Clintons left the White House at the end of Bill's second term, Hillary's approval rating was at an all-time high. After the 2008 election, she took the post as Secretary of State at the request of President Barack Obama.

Hillary's personal life is a key part of her political life. Should Hillary become president, Bill would become the first First Husband in the history of the White House.

Bill Clinton

Although this book is about Hillary Clinton and the lies she perpetrates in cover-ups to advance her political career, it must be noted her husband was the center of many damaging allegations which will briefly be discussed here. In return, Hillary has since used Bill's influence to offset and minimize charges against her.

The former 42nd President of the United States has the distinction of having been accused by several women of sexual assault. It is interesting to note that almost all of these allegations surfaced only after he attained the position of president and that the alleged victims have been harassed as a result of coming forth.

By no means is this a complete list. Here are a number of historical allegations of indecent incidents:

In 1969, Eileen Wellstone was 19 when she met Bill at a pub near Oxford while he was a student there. She claims sexual assault. A retired State Department employee confirmed that he spoke with the girl's family and filed a report. Bill Clinton admitted to having sex with her claiming it was consensual. Amazingly, the girl's family declined to press charges.

In 1972, a 22-year-old woman, who requested to remain anonymous, told campus police at Yale University that she was sexually assaulted by Bill Clinton at the college, but no charges were ever filed.

In 1974, a female student, who has declined to go on record, at the University of Arkansas alleged that her law school instructor Bill Clinton tried to prevent her from leaving his office. She stated he groped her and forced his hand inside her blouse. She complained to her advisor who confronted Bill Clinton, who asserted the student initiated acts with him. Shortly after the incident, the student left the school. There have also been several other former students that have confirmed the incident in confidential interviews and stated there were other reports of Bill Clinton attempting to force himself on female students.

In 1978, Juanita Broaddrick, a volunteer in Bill Clinton's campaign for governor, said he brutally raped her. White House attorneys report this was consensual.

From 1978-1980, state troopers who were assigned to protect Governor Clinton were aware of at least seven complaints from women on whom Bill Clinton forced himself or attempted to use force sexually. One former trooper told how they would escort women to Bill Clinton's hotel room after political events, frequently more than one in an evening.

In 1979, Carolyn Moffet met Bill Clinton at a political fundraiser and then got invited to meet the Governor at his hotel room. She was escorted to his hotel room by a state trooper and, when in the room, saw him sitting on a couch wearing only an undershirt. He allegedly pointed to his genitalia and ordered her to engage in oral sex. She refused, and he became angry grabbing her head and forcing it into his lap. She pulled away and ran from the room. A former neighbor of hers said afterward she would receive harassing phone calls.

Elizabeth Ward was a Miss Arkansas who won Miss America in 1982. She told her friends she was forced to have sex with Bill Clinton. Ward, now married, told an interviewer she did have consensual sex with Bill Clinton, but close friends of Ward maintain she privately feels he forced himself on her.

Paula Jones worked as an Arkansas state worker. She filed a sexual harassment case against Bill Clinton after the then-Governor made a demand for oral sex in a Little Rock hotel room. Bill Clinton settled the case with Jones in 1998 for an $850,000 cash payment, which just goes to prove it really happened and he wanted it to go away.

Sandra Allen James claims she was invited to Bill Clinton's hotel room (is there a trend here?) where he pinned her to the wall while he stuck his hand up her dress. At this point, she screamed so loud the state trooper stationed outside the door banged on it asking if everything was all okay. Bill Clinton then released her, and she ran out of the room. She reported the incident to her boss who advised her to keep quiet if she wanted to keep her job. She says she later learned other women suffered the same fate. She allegedly would not go forward claiming the Clinton White House destroys people who get in their way.

In 1992, Christy Zercher was a flight attendant on a leased campaign plane. She says Bill exposed himself to her and grabbed her breasts while making explicit remarks about oral sex. An ABC News video on the plane shows an inebriated Bill Clinton with his hand between another flight attendant's legs. Zercher said White House attorney

Bruce Lindsey pressured her not to go public about the assault.

In 1993, Kathleen Willey was a White House volunteer who reported that Bill Clinton grabbed her, fondled her breast, and pressed her hand against his genitals. She told her story in a 60 Minutes interview and alleged she became a target of a White House-directed smear campaign after going public.

Over 30 interviews were made with former state troopers, retired Arkansas state employees, and former University of Arkansas and Yale students who refuse to go public out of fear.
The resounding tone is that Bill has a problem treating women as sex toys for his pleasure. He does whatever he wants, and Hillary does her best to help cover up for the sake of power and greed. This truly is a marriage of convenience.

Retaliation Detailed

In retaliation for making accusations about the indecent assault, the Clintons have been said to have hired private investigators to try and expose their adversaries. Threats, scare tactics, and stalking have been confirmed by a number of the former accusers who have been willing to come forth and speak out about the unfairness.

It is asserted that Hillary orchestrated a campaign of harassment and intimidation that fits a pattern described by other women.

The only allegations Bill admits to are the affairs with Gennifer Flowers and Monica Lewinsky.

Mistakes were made by the accuser Broaddrick, who continued to support Bill Clinton at public events after being raped. Broaddrick also had signed a statement saying she did not have sex with Bill Clinton. Afterward, she said she did not want to testify publicly about the details of such a horrific event.

Broaddrick resurfaced with Hillary's 2016 presidential campaign stating Hillary knew what happened and how she threatened Broaddrick to keep silent. Broaddrick gave interviews in 2015 because she was angered by Hillary's statements that victims of sexual crimes should be believed. To Broaddrick, there was the public side of Hillary and the dark side that she faced when she went public.

Dolly Kyle Browning, a lawyer in Texas, made a deposition as part of the Paula Jones case. She was a childhood classmate of Bill and knew him since age 11. She also had an affair with him for approximately 18 years. When she began writing a novel that outlined the affair, she alleged Bill tried to halt its publication.

The Paula Jones case against Bill alleging sexual harassment is what put him under oath to testify about his sexual history. It was here he denied having had an affair with Monica Lewinsky. This denial is what led to his impeachment for perjury and obstruction of justice.

In 1998, Kathleen Willey came forth in the Paula Jones case and alleged Bill Clinton assaulted her in the White House in 1993. Kenneth Starr granted her immunity for her testimony in his separate inquiry.

Linda Tripp, a White House staffer, testified that Willey's sexual contact with Bill Clinton was consensual. Almost ironically, Willey's second husband, Edward E. Willey Jr., was found dead from a gunshot wound on the exact same day she claimed Bill Clinton's sexual misconduct took place. His death was determined to be a suicide by investigators. She has written a book and been interviewed on 60 Minutes talking about her suspicions that the Clintons were somehow involved in the death of her former husband, and she details the similarities to the alleged suicide of Vince Foster, including how both deaths occurred in close proximity to each other in the state of Virginia. Kenneth Starr dismissed the Willey case due to insufficient evidence.

During the Paula Jones trial, Gennifer Flowers revealed her 12-year affair with Bill, who testified under oath that he had sexual relations with her. For once he came clean.

Other allegations have come out with all of them saying the same thing over and over which is that Bill had relationships with them or had propositioned them. He is often labeled as a predator, but perhaps a better label for him would be a sex addict who needs professional help.

Hillary has been shown as an accessory in that she knew about the misconduct but did nothing, thus serving as an enabler. He knew he could do it and that she would help cover for him without question. Given this fact, and that everyone in the country has seen the stories of Bill's "exploits" on television, it's a wonder people believe her rantings about fairness for women involved in sexual assault allegations.

In his defense, Hillary also uses religion to compare Bill to the Prodigal Son—that he may be taken back despite his indiscretions. Even though the public has passed their judgment on Bill over the decades, she still stands behind him, at least when in public view.

How a woman can remain with and be supportive of a man who has done what he has, repeatedly, raises questions of motive. There are more reports than the ones listed here showing dozens upon dozens of women, most of whom want to remain nameless, who have suffered by his aggressions. It is likely that Hillary may need Bill more than Bill needs Hillary. Bill has always been a better campaigner than Hillary. But this time, it is Hillary that wants to get elected. That may be one of the driving forces that keeps them together. It seems less likely that she would be able to run for president as a divorced woman. There is also, of course, the power and money that they share through the Clinton Foundation. That may be another factor that keeps them together.

USING THE IRS

Chapter 9

The Internal Revenue Service may have been used, or abused, for corrupt means and to harass political enemies. Back in the day, tax evasion was what they used to convict Al Capone.

Audit Your Enemies

During Bill Clinton's terms in office, the IRS conducted audits against individuals and groups who had brought either legal scandals to light for the Administration or had criticized the President or his policies.

Among the groups audited were the National Rifle Association, the Heritage Foundation, the Concerned Women of America, National Review, Citizens Against Government Waste, the National Center for Public Policy Research, American Spectator (which was burglarized three times), the American Policy Center, Citizens for Honest Government, the American Cause, David Horowitz's Center for the Study of Popular Culture, the Progress & Freedom Foundation, and the Western Journalism Center.

Individuals who were audited after they went public against Clinton include ex-lovers Liz Ward Gracen and Gennifer Flowers, sexual assault accusers Juanita Broaddrick and Paula Jones, Bill Dale, a fired White House Travel Office Director; and attorney Kent Masterson Brown. Bill O'Reilly of

FOX News and critic of the Clintons said he was audited three times.

IRS Under Obama

When Hillary served under Obama as Secretary of State, Obama may have learned from Hillary how to use the IRS. The Obama Administration seems to have done a much better job of utilizing the IRS for attacking the Tea Party Republicans than the Clintons ever did. The Obama Administration used the power of the IRS to prevent the formation of Tea Party organizations for years. If a group cannot operate, it simply cannot be effective.

Max Vanguard

HEALTH CARE REFORM
1993

Chapter 10

In his quest for the presidency during his 1992 campaign, Bill Clinton focused on a healthcare reform package that would provide healthcare to all Americans.

Immediately after being sworn into office in 1993, the first steps were put into motion for The Clinton Health Care Plan. Bill set up the Task Force on National Health Care Reform and appointed Hillary as the Chair to devise and implement the plan.

The idea was to mandate employers to provide coverage to all their employees through closely regulated health maintenance organizations (HMOs). Controversial processes surfaced and resulted in litigation primarily from the Association of American Physicians and Surgeons.

In short, the bill was over 1,000 pages long and required each U.S. citizen and permanent resident alien to be enrolled in one of the qualified health plans. Dis-enrollment was forbidden until coverage was in place by another plan to ensure there was continuous coverage. It also listed the coverage and annual out-of-pocket expenses for each plan with the provision there would be no cost for people below a certain set income level. The act listed funding to be allocated to the states for the administration of this plan, beginning at 38.3 billion in 2003.

Secrets Behind Closed Doors

In 1993, Hillary was involved in litigation over secret proceedings. The exact details of these closed-door meetings of the Health Care Task Force have never been revealed. The U.S. Court of Appeals for the D.C. Circuit reviewed the issue of whether Hillary was in violation of the Federal Advisory Committee Act (FACA) which requires openness in affairs where the government is involved. The White House argued that Article II of the U.S. Constitution made it unconstitutional to apply FACA to her involvement with the Task Force. Ultimately, she was absolved, in that, as First Lady, she was no longer a private citizen, but a government official.

In February 1993, a lawsuit was filed against Hillary by the Association of American Physicians and Surgeons (AAPS) and several other groups with a vested interest in gaining access to the list of task force members. This information was released when the AAPS won and in addition, they were awarded a sum to cover their legal costs in the suit.

The End Result
Opponents criticized the bill as restrictive of patient choice and overly bureaucratic, unofficially calling it "Hillarycare" due to her involvement as Task Force Chair.

Failure

By September 1994, Senate Majority Leader George J. Mitchell tried a final compromise to save the bill. The plan had failed. With the plan scrapped, Bill Clinton's political position was weakened. This was a major blow for both Bill and Hillary.

Max Vanguard

CHINAGATE

Chapter 11

Chinagate, which is part of Commercegate, was a campaign fundraising scandal in which Hillary was very involved.

Re-election Funding

When Bill was running for re-election in 1996, he was the recipient of large sums of donations by high-tech companies eager to do business with China. The premise is that they also took bribes from the Chinese who were interested in opening the door to high-tech information as well.

A scheme allegedly cooked up by Hillary was for then-Secretary of Commerce Ron Brown to sell seats, under the guise of campaign contributions, on taxpayer-funded trade missions. Judicial Watch, a conservative organization, brought a legal case seeking to find out the truth about Chinagate. The Clinton Administration sought to destroy documents related to Chinagate so that Judicial Watch would not find any smoking gun.

Confidante and business partner to Ron Brown, Nolanda Hill, testified in court that Hillary Clinton was the mastermind behind a scheme to sell seats for campaign contributions on China trade missions that Secretary Ron Brown was to organize through the commerce department. Further, Nolanda Hill said that the Clinton Administration told Brown to delay the case by withholding sensitive documents before the 1996 elections and to find a way not to comply with the court's orders. There were numerous investigations into Chinagate: congressional, Justice Department, Federal Election Commission, and FBI cases. Ron Brown's Commerce Department and Ron himself were the targets of a number of these investigations. Ron Brown subsequently died on an unrelated commerce trip to Bosnia that Hillary Clinton sent him on. There will be a whole chapter on Ron Brown later in this book.

A larger and more sinister plan was hatched by the Clinton Administration and CEO Bernard Schwartz of Loral Space & Communications Ltd. The plan was to transfer U.S. missile technology to China to help with Bill Clinton's 1996 presidential campaign. Schwartz donated about $1.5 million to democrats including Bill Clinton. In return, Schwartz got approval from the Clinton Administration State Department to have satellites launched from China. The transfer of technology advanced China's missile program by decades and put money into the Clinton-Gore re-election campaign.

Investigations found that Clinton Administration officials had falsified testimony and deliberately destroyed and concealed records regarding the trade missions.

The Department of Justice investigation found that over 100 people that were somehow connected to the scandal had either fled the country or would plead the Fifth Amendment to avoid testifying.

With no evidence, Federal charges of racketeering were never brought.

As the investigation of this scandal was underway, congressional hearings arose until democrats found evidence of illegal republican fundraising and the "new" Monica Lewinsky case was found to distract the country with another one of Bill's juicy sex scandals.

Much later in 2006, an appellate court upheld an award of $900,000 to Judicial Watch as payment for their legal fees to bring this case to court on behalf of Loral shareholders.

RONALD H. BROWN

Chapter 12

It was on April 3, 1996, that Commerce Secretary Ron Brown died along with 34 others when their Air Force plane crashed into a mountainside.

Ironically, Hillary had made an unplanned stop in Bosnia a few days before Brown's fatal final flight was to leave that very airport and, there are massive amounts of circumstantial evidence that the Clintons were involved. There is no evidence Islamic or any sort of other terrorists killed Brown, but there is speculation of sabotage from the quick and ineffectual investigation that was done.

The back story is that Brown himself knew too much and was also being investigated for corruption stemming from his involvement in Chinagate. He had damning evidence about all the scandals since Whitewater. He would have been able to provide a direct trail of money which led to Bill and Hillary Clinton. There is even speculation that he confronted the Clintons that he would go public about the Chinagate scandal.

Brown was allegedly Clinton's enforcer with regard to bringing Iranian Muslims and their weapons into the Bosnian war.

The Clintons had ordered Brown to withhold documents requested in the Chinagate investigations. Only weeks before his untimely death, Brown started going to church. When Brown was called to testify in an investigation about himself, he knew he was in serious trouble. He knew the Clintons and what they were capable of. He was scared for his life and the life of Nolanda Hill, his business associate, confidante, and possible lover.

Brown's last days were spent trying to protect his son from going to prison by threatening to expose the White House's unknown Asian (Chinagate) fundraising scheme in which Brown played a major role.

It's clear Brown was pulled into involvement and used like a number of other people as pawns in a scheme put together by Hillary to help Bill. When Bill was out in front as president, she was lurking somewhere in the background making sure any documents or people that could convict them were eliminated to keep control of the power they had and all the money that came with it.

On this trip to Bosnia, Brown was also assigned to broker a deal with the President of Croatia, Franjo Tudjman, and Enron Corporation, as there was big money to be made in getting these two together.

Accident or Assassination?
Here are the facts. Brown's last flight came only six months after the insertion of American troops into Bosnia. The Enron executives had their own plane. The Air Force investigation notes the plane inexplicably deviated almost two miles inland,

which is highly unusual. It is the first time the safety portion of the investigation of a downed plane was not allowed to be conducted. Only the accident phase was to be investigated.

There is evidence that the plane lost electrical power when it was seven miles away from where it crashed into the mountains, and the plane was about 2500 feet above the Adriatic Sea. The point at which the electrical power went out was when the plane was flying over water on its approach to Dubrovnik Airport. Why is it believed that there was an electrical power loss in the airplane? There are at least three reasons. First, the tower lost voice contact with the plane. There is a split radar system that watches the approach of the plane. This system uses the transponder of the airplane to track the location of the plane. When the electrical system goes out, the plane transponder also stops. There was a United States AWACS plane in the area that was also tracking Ron Brown's plane by its transponder. The AWACS aircraft stopped tracking Ron Brown's plane at the same time Dubrovnik was not able to track the aircraft. This would seem to rule out a failure of the equipment at Dubrovnik and point to a total electrical failure on the plane. The flight controls and the electrical wires are all run through the same conduit. If the electrical system was disabled for two different systems (voice and transponder), then it is likely that the plane lost flight control as well and just continued on the general course it was on and crashed in the mountains.

The Clinton Administration put out a new story about how the plane crashed in "the worst storm in a decade." This line was picked up by numerous media outlets like Time and Newsweek. However, the weather was not that bad. There was light rain and visibility of five miles with clouds at 2000 feet.

Three days after the CT-43 crash, the Croatian responsible for the airport's navigation system was found with a bullet to the chest. His death was ruled a suicide. This was only two days before his scheduled interview with the Air Force. There is another theory on how the plane crashed. Sources state the plane was purposely guided into the mountainside. Use of one non-directional beacon to guide the plane from takeoff to a certain area and turn it off when a second beacon would immediately turn on and lead the plane to crash it into the mountainside. The Croatian responsible may have been forced to cooperate at gunpoint and then killed to cover up anything he might say to the U.S. Air Force.

 It was reported on Croatian TV and other media that the black boxes from the crashed plane had been recovered and turned over to American authorities. All commercial models of that aircraft come with flight recorders, but the Clinton Administration claimed that this aircraft had no black boxes.

There was a survivor found at the site of the CT-43 (Modified Boeing 737) crash. Shelly Kelly, a stewardess, had survived possibly because she was in the tail of the plane. She was moving and conscious and evacuated by helicopter to a hospital. She was said to have died en route to the hospital, and the cause of death was a broken neck. This was very suspicious, and her death would have been required to cover up what actually happened to the aircraft.

Initial examination of Brown's body by no fewer than three Armed Forces pathologists and a forensic photographer shows a head wound that looks like a bullet hole but with no exit wound. Brown's family was not informed of the matter. Head X-rays were lost. Orders by the Administration were issued such that no autopsy or forensic tests were to be performed. The death certificate notes cause of death as multiple blunt force injuries to the head and Brown was the only one on the flight to have a head wound.

A copy of the head X-rays was discovered by Chris Ruddy when he found Dr. Cogswell was using them as an example in one of the Armed Forces lectures for pathologists. The X-rays clearly showed metal fragments in the brain that were consistent with a gunshot to the top of his head because of the inward beveling hole on the head and the "snowstorm" of metal fragments. When Chris Ruddy started to write articles about the death of

Ron Brown, a gag order was placed on Dr. Cogswell and Dr. Hause by the Clinton Administration.
President Clinton ordered the cremation of all victims. This would ensure that any evidence left in the bodies would be destroyed. Bill Clinton also took two days to honor Ron Brown after he died. Nobody would question the possible involvement of one who spends a great deal of time to honor a victim.

The ordered lack of customary procedure during the Ron Brown plane crash investigation shows a desperate attempt to hide the facts. When you consider all of the following, this was clearly not what it was reported as:

1.• Ron Brown was being investigated for his involvement in Chinagate.
2.• Ron Brown was about to go public or talk to investigators.
3.• Hillary was the alleged mastermind behind Chinagate.
4.• Hillary was in Bosnia at the same airfield where Ron Brown's plane took off just before it crashed, only three days earlier.
5.• The Croatian government insisted on a Dubrovnik stop just 36 hours before Ron Brown's scheduled landing.
6.• The Air Force is told by the Clinton Administration to skip the initial investigation of why the plane crashed and just assume it was an accident.

7.• Enron executives take their own plane.

8.• Three days after the crash, a Croatian navigational engineer is found dead with a bullet in his chest. The death is ruled a suicide.

9.• X-rays of Ron Brown's head show a gunshot to the head.

10.• Pathologists who report the gunshot finding have a gag order placed on them.

11.• The Air Force cannot explain why the plane made a two-mile deviation into the mountains and crashed.

12.• Possible sabotage of the plane's electrical system.

13.• Possible Dubrovnik navigational system sabotage.

14.• The Clinton Administration did not tell the truth about the weather around Dubrovnik. They appeared to try and make it much worse than it was.

15.• President Clinton orders the cremation of all bodies.

16.• A passenger on the plane survives but on the way to the hospital dies due to a broken neck.

17.• Black boxes from the plane are recovered but then the Clinton Administration tells us there were no black boxes on that plane.

How many lies do you have to hear before you realize that something very, very creepy and devious is going on here? Ask yourself this: Who had the most to gain from the death of Ron Brown?

Max Vanguard

HILLARY UNDER FIRE IN BOSNIA

Chapter 13

In 1996, Hillary as First Lady, along with daughter Chelsea, made a trip to Bosnia. On more than one occasion, she embellishes her story stating they landed under sniper fire and had to run with their heads down for cover. News footage of the event shows she lied about the incident. It was rainy, and she appeared to keep her head down somewhat, but there was no sniper fire, and they didn't run for cover.

This is a perfect example of how a politician will say anything to elicit a desired response.

Almost ironically, this was only several days before Ron Brown would die on a plane that left that same airfield and would crash into a mountainside.

Some people are compulsive liars and can't stop. They exaggerate the truth to the extent that the majority calls it a lie. The filters of their brains work differently. It doesn't make it right; it's just a fact. When caught, they realize the mistake and cover it up as best they can with excuses like they can't remember, they made a mistake, or they make up another lie that they had never said it to begin with.

Max Vanguard

EMAIL GATE

Chapter 14

In early 2015, a newspaper report revealed Secretary of State Hillary Clinton used her own private email server, rather than the one issued to her by the government. Investigations also reveal that the day of her first Senate hearing to become Secretary of State, Hillary Clinton or an associate purchased another private email server which was set up in her Chappaqua, New York, home. The incident gained widespread attention due to security concerns over possible hacking or surveillance.

Personal Server

In total, there were 62,320 emails at risk that Hillary Clinton had sent or received on the private email account in question. The separate server was allegedly set up as a matter of convenience so that she would only need to carry one device, not two. In retrospect, she admits it would have been better to have used a second email account and a second phone.

Questions remain as to whether Hillary Clinton signed Form OF-109, a standard document declaring she turned over all work-related records, upon her February 2013 resignation. After searching, the State Department stated it had no record that Hillary Clinton signed the form and was fairly certain she did not. In the research it was found that neither of her two immediate predecessors signed the forms. The form text warns individuals signing it that falsification is subject to criminal penalties under Section 1001 of Title 18. How convenient she didn't sign it.

Potential Mishandling of Classified Information

It was shown that the Inspectors General of the Intelligence Community and the State Department concluded there were hundreds of instances of classified information in the emails that originated from U.S. intelligence agencies, such as the CIA and the NSA.

Hillary can blame all the aides she wants as scapegoats, but the fact remains, she was in charge the whole time. It was all done under her direction. Having classified information on your private server is a "red flag."

It all began when the Intelligence Community Inspector General was brought in on a referral about Secretary Clinton's use of various personal email servers that she purchased during her time as Secretary of State. Also, various personal transmitting devices were used. The focus of the investigation was on whether any classified information was transmitted to or from her personal server system.

The investigation of approximately 30,000 emails at this point looked for evidence of classified information being improperly transmitted or stored on her personal email server. Emails and email chains were determined to be of a classified nature, some even Top Secret. Some emails that were not of a classified nature at the time have since been elevated and thus "up-classified" to where they are now confidential information.

Such an act of mishandling classified information, intentionally or by gross negligence, is a direct violation of a federal statute and is a felony. A second statute makes it a misdemeanor to knowingly remove classified information from such government systems or storage facilities.

Also investigated was whether there was evidence of computer hacking of the personal email server by any foreign entity or some other hostile group. Additionally, interviews were conducted of everyone who could have been involved, such as technical people, staff, anyone who sent her emails, and Clinton herself.

Extensive work was done to look for signs of hacking. It was noted, no evidence of intentional deletion to conceal, misconduct, or hacking was found, but it was possible information was hacked.'
No case of criminal or willful mishandling or misconduct was found, and no charges were brought on Hillary Clinton. However, FBI Director

Comey did strongly reprimand her for breaking the rules and that she should have known better. For her to get off with only a stern lecture shows the power associated through decades of political involvement, making connections with the right people which have apparently paid off. He also applied a double standard that someone else in this same situation would face charges, which makes no sense. Republicans as well as U.S. citizens in general were very upset at all of this, especially in view of the elections.

The problem with this is that her professional business is to be a trusted government employee whose primary goal is to make decisions to help keep this country secure. Hillary breached that trust by using a personal server. FBI investigations have uncovered many emails of a classified nature, and now we are finding some have even been up-classified to Top Secret, containing information sensitive to this nation's security.

Experts agree that the ramifications are huge and that in time they will become more apparent as the information that was hacked gets used against us.
If Hillary can't properly manage a tool as simple as email, how can she manage the job of president, or at this point, any other political office? The answer is she can't. Her flat answers reek of scandal and conspiracy.

The bottom line is that she should have known better as the intelligent (Yale Law School grad) government veteran that she is, and all she has to say is, "I made a mistake."

How many people have been fired for making less of a mistake, like Democratic National Convention Chair Wasserman Schultz who just resigned over pressure from the email fall-out?

For Comey to add that the State Department shared fault in the matter, apparently for not finding this out by themselves, is logical but not realistic. Who in their right mind would look into Hillary Clinton's (of all people) email use? Especially with a track record of bad things that happened to people who did stand up.

Even Hillary's allegations of trying to keep her personal business personal looks like she is trying to hide something. Wouldn't a secured government server be the securest place to keep any information? It's obvious no one was looking at her government account, or they would have found nothing as it was all on the personal server. What does she have to hide anyway, more scandals?

An interesting angle is if Hillary lied about not knowing that the private email server was a mistake. Speculating it was done on purpose, was the motive to pass classified information done in order to gain power and money? There is more to it all than meets the eye. If this is how Hillary handles her current post, then how will she improve if she becomes president when there is more at stake. What we are seeing is just the tip of the iceberg.

TRAVELGATE

Chapter 15

This was a scandal about how the Clintons decided to make changes when they first came to the White House. One of the changes they made was to fire the White House travel office staff in order to hire friends and relatives. Although some may consider this a noble gesture of putting family and friends first, it should be noted how unprofessionally this was done. None of the employees was given any notice, and they were fired on the spot after having worked in their positions for a good many years.

An investigation was made, and five employees were put on administrative leave initially, then given other jobs in government as a consolation.

The travel office stems from the days of Andrew Jackson and serves to this day as the office that books the transportation of the White House Press Corps.

When protests were made about the firing decisions, Hillary allegedly requested the FBI do an investigation on Billy Dale, the former head of the White House travel office, for embezzlement. Dale was later audited by the IRS, which found he was not guilty, a common thing to happen to anyone crossing the path of the Clintons. His position was allegedly taken over by a cousin of Bill Clinton.

As a result of Independent Counsel Robert Ray's investigation in 2000, it was found that Hillary made statements that were factually false. It was not determined if she had done so intentionally. As any good lawyer knows, it is proving the intent to lie, mislead, or cover up that makes it a chargeable offense. Mere ignorance is only reprimanded.

Max Vanguard

<hr>

BENGHAZI

<hr>

Chapter 16

On Sept. 11, 2012, U.S. Ambassador J. Christopher Stevens, U.S. Foreign Service Information Management Officer Sean Smith, and CIA contractors, Tyrone Woods and Glen Doherty, were killed by Islamic militants who attacked the American diplomatic compound in Benghazi, Libya. Delayed response time resulted in these deaths in which two separate attacks were made. In fact, Ambassador Stevens' diary notes his concern regarding the lack of security and the requests for help that went unanswered.

The first American troops arrived after it was all over. It was the first time since 1979 that an American ambassador had been killed.

It was during this time that Hillary Clinton was the Secretary of State. The political instability of the area was growing, and repeated requests were made for additional security. The alarming fact is that in the months leading up to the attacks, Hillary's State Department actually cut security in Libya despite the heated situation.

Hindsight is always 20/20, but it can clearly be seen that Hillary's lack of providing sufficient security is what led to the numerous requests made for additional security.

The Back Story

Islamic militants were brought in, along with many weapons, for the 2011 Libyan Civil War that killed the then-leader of that country, Muammar Gaddafi. Ambassador Stevens was the first liaison with the party leading the revolution.
The aftermath left the country unstable with many small attacks going on daily. Three days before the siege there were reports of deteriorating security in the area of the compound.

Controversy surrounds the event as the temporary compound did not meet normal security specifications.

The Islamic militants came in trucks with the logo Ansar al-Sharia, a group working with the local government to provide security. They were heavily armed with AK-47s, grenades, other assault weapons, and cans of diesel fuel.

At first, the U.S. claimed the attacks were in response to a controversial video titled "Innocence of Muslims." This was an anti-Muslim film serving to spark protests. The U.S. mistakenly claimed it was these protests that led to the Benghazi compound attack to avoid making the attack look like an act of terrorism. However, Libyans interviewed stated no such protests occurred. Hillary's focus has remained that the video caused all this to happen, which does nothing to answer for her Department's lack of timely response that may have saved Americans.

Hillary also sent an email to her daughter telling her that terrorists were responsible but then told Americans that the attack was due to the movie. But Hillary should not take all the blame for this. President Obama was up for re-election, and he wanted Americans to believe this was an attack from a spontaneous demonstration and not a terrorist attack.

The assault wasn't sophisticated, but it was obvious the attackers had trained together and had clear orders on how to proceed. It was evident they had excellent intelligence, knowing how to get to different access points in the ambassador's compound and how to cut off the security guards.

What did happen is Special-Ops-trained independent security forces on assignment caught wind of the cries for assistance and responded on their own from another location. Traveling from Tripoli to Benghazi, they provided support during the two attacks.

Emails confirm protective forces could have moved swiftly to Benghazi if given the green light to do so. Hillary Clinton maintains other State Department professionals under her were assigned to make the decisions regarding security requests.

Adding to the issues is the fact that it took the FBI over three weeks to get to the Benghazi consulate to find only "cold" evidence. This made it much more difficult to investigate, and it took a long time before suspects in the slaying were identified and arrested.

Hillary's lack of response to send security to aid Stevens and the other Americans is morally reprehensible. It is the duty of the Secretary of State to decide to either secure the permission of another country for U.S. military to enter, or simply enter without permission.

Allegedly, part of the delay in sending help was because the State Department wasted time trying to figure out if military or civilian clothes should be worn, and if the vehicles they use should have identifiable U.S. markings. The idea concerning diplomacy was part of what held up the response.

Connection to Email Controversy

A recently discovered hidden email chain revealed how only hours after the siege began, troops could have immediately gone to Benghazi. Even with the classified information redacted, it is obvious the military was waiting for the orders to proceed, but no such order came. The mere fact this email was withheld, and for so long, only underscores that this was a scandal.

CLINTON ACCOUNTING WHILE AT THE STATE DEPARTMENT

Chapter 17

Another scandal involves accounting, where the State Department under Hillary Clinton could not account for about six billion dollars' worth of contracts made during the previous six years. Why it took six years to look into this to begin with is still a mystery.

State Department Accounting Investigation

In 2014, the Office of the Inspector General made an investigation and audit with a report noting the Department's failure to properly maintain the contract files along with inadequate contract control which thereby created financial risk.

Request for Documents

Also, when the Associated Press (AP) requested that the State Department turn over documents via the Freedom of Information Act (FOIA), they were kindly told they were too busy to respond at that time, but would provide them as soon as possible.

As can be deduced, there seemed to be deliberate withholding of possible evidence—as well as an effort to run the clock out of time—containing information that would make Hillary look bad in her initial stages of running for president in 2016. In the past, information had been "lost" and then later "found." As any good lawyer knows, you need evidence to convict.

The Cash Cow – The Clinton Foundation

There was an ethics agreement formed at the beginning of Hillary's term in the State Department between the State Department, Bill, and the Clinton Foundation that disclosure of details of donations be made as a means of "checks and balances."
Donations from foreign governments poured in. Bill had proven himself to be a prolific public speaker and savvy in meeting with foreign leaders and telling them things to entice them into contributing to such a cause.

The result is the Clinton Foundation had failed to disclose donors as agreed. Again, we see Hillary involved in breaking the rules and helping herself and Bill to make more money.

Another questionable donation was for $500,000 from Algeria in 2010, for earthquake relief in Haiti. This should have received a special ethics review due to the fact that it was not included in the continuation provision. The donation was made at the same time lobbying efforts of the State Department were undertaken by Algeria regarding their human rights record. In essence it was a payoff so as not to receive an unfavorable grade by Hillary's department on such a sensitive issue.

An analysis of records shows the State Department approved of almost all of Bill Clinton's speaking engagements although they lacked information about the value and links between them and possible donations. This shows Bill had carte blanche to make money any way he could for the Clinton Foundation with no obstacles. Also, the Clintons do not seem concerned about such things as pesky record keeping, as has been shown in the past.

During the period of 2009 through 2013, Rosatom, a Russian atomic energy agency, acquired Canadian uranium mining company Uranium One. This acquisition is interesting as Uranium One has rights to one-fifth of uranium mined in the U.S. Particularly sensitive is the fact this now goes to Russia. For the acquisition to be approved there had to be agreement between the Canadian government and a number of U.S. governmental bodies, one of which was the State Department. During the acquisition, Uranium One's chairman's family foundation conveniently made a multi-million-dollar donation to the Clinton Foundation. Bill Clinton also received a $500,000 payment from a Russian investment bank for making a speech in Moscow. Despite the ethics agreement, the donations were not disclosed by the Clinton Foundation or the State Department. As sneaky as it may have been, in this case, the donations going through the Canadian affiliate absolved the ethics agreement made. Although questions were raised there was no evidence of influence by Hillary in her official role. And let's not forget the illegal tax write-offs from the losses.

Max Vanguard

<hr>

HILLARY ON WOMEN'S RIGHTS

Chapter 18

Republicans, like Carly Fiorina, argue that it is hypocritical for Hillary Clinton to present herself as a champion of women's rights while the Clinton Foundation accepts major donations from countries like Saudi Arabia who do not have a very good record in their treatment of women.

Another knock on her is the lack of accomplishment on her resume toward supporting women. So far, all she has done is talk on the subject, but, talk is something. Words spoken and written are the tools used by diplomats, presidents, and journalists.

Still, whether she talked enough, forcefully and when it mattered, is a fair question. There is not much talk when it comes to the masses of women who risk coming forth with allegations against her husband, Bill.

She stood by Bill and he was a womanizer and she did nothing about that in defense of women. By sticking by him, she seems to condone his actions treating women with little or no respect. In fact, when it comes to her private life, she is not all that aggressive in her defense of women, as evidenced by what she said of Monica Lewinsky as a "narcissistic loony toon."

There is also the case of her 1975 defense of a 41-year-old man who allegedly raped a 12-year-old girl. Her tone on the audio interview is that she had a job to do and did it. All the evidence backed her client, whom she did not choose to defend. It was apparently her good lawyering that served to get a criminal off the hook.

In her favor, there is a report Hillary Clinton had ignored security concerns to visit refugees and survivors of sexual assault in the Democratic Republic of Congo back in 2009.

Friends and aides say while Hillary Clinton was on vacation that summer she sent many emails—albeit from her personal account—to get the department focused on the matter. Then, she dispatched some of her aides to determine what, if anything, could be done to make it more difficult for warlords to use the tactics of assault as a weapon of war and to warn camps of imminent invasions should they persist in using these tactics.

The efforts fell short mainly due to legal hurdles and from the non-cooperation of the Congolese government. But, Hillary Clinton's personal anguish and involvement convinced them that protecting women from violence was very important to her.

To her credit, Hillary Clinton was behind the adoption of a U.N. resolution that laid out guidelines for international response when sexual assault was discovered in war-torn areas.

During her speech at the Fourth World Conference on Women in Beijing in 1995, she fiercely argued how it was not acceptable to discuss women's rights as separate from human rights.

As is typical to Hillary's mindset, she took a calculated risk in each case, and had a specific, achievable goal in mind.

Max Vanguard

<hr>

HILLARY FOR PRESIDENT

Chapter 19

Superdelegates

Established in 1984, a superdelegate is basically a current or former democratic politician to the Democratic National Convention who is seated automatically and can support any candidate for the presidential nomination, and even switch sides. To have their vote count, they must attend and vote at the convention. The candidate with the most superdelegates has historically been a reliable indicator of who becomes the nominee.

Although they don't necessarily reflect the will of the people in their state, it does help to consider the opinion of those who elected them.

Back in 2008, Hillary Clinton led Obama by about 100 superdelegates, but that advantage shrank after Obama held a sustained advantage of pledged delegates. And in the end it was Obama who overtook her in superdelegates by the end of the primary season.

By the Numbers

Superdelegates make up 15 percent of all delegates, currently 714 out of 4,765, and are believed to be the path to winning the Democratic nomination. Superdelegates have never changed the outcome of the primary season.

The essence of this system in this election shows Hillary Clinton had a 15% head start over Sanders, which has him and others crying "foul." Obviously, during Hillary Clinton's time in politics she has built relationships with the right insiders who help influence this type of advantage.

Arguments are that this is what is, and has been, wrong with Washington—too many systems in place that end up keeping things as they are, as party roots run deep. Also, a candidate's electability by the rest of the country is an important factor the superdelegate keeps in mind.

Just another way Hillary uses her influence to get what she wants.

EMAIL CONTROVERSY
AFTERMATH

Chapter 20

Apparently, 22 million files of individuals who applied for security clearances were stolen by Red China. These files contain in-depth electronic questionnaires (called EQIPs or EPSQs) from the applicants. Personal information such as marital status, criminal background, drug use/abuse, and more complete the file. Obviously, the loss of this critical information is devastating. In the wrong hands it can be used to blackmail a cleared individual, thus compromising security greatly.

The OPM Hack

The Office of Personnel Management (OPM) was hacked into, allegedly a result of Hillary Clinton's personal email server at her New York home.
The seriousness is such that the CIA pulled its agents out of Beijing for safety reasons. Also at risk are current and future military operations. It is predicted the compromised position we are now in could soon be revealed in tragic attacks.

The scope of risk is far-reaching, as it is believed many foreign intelligence agencies from other countries, including Russia, have also collected a virtual treasure trove of sensitive information vital to our national security.

In fact, as far back as 2011, Hillary's Chief of Staff, Cheryl Mills, warned her of the danger of using a personal email server. It is now coming to light that everyone involved with Hillary who was aware of the use of the personal server usage knew it was a violation and how it endangered national security.

New reports state there were an estimated 400 classified email messages on Hillary's personal server, with each carrying a felony violation subject to imprisonment of up to ten years.

Interestingly enough, a democratic operative admitted knowing Hillary used her personal server to avoid scrutiny of her shameful backroom activities.

The FBI investigated whether Hillary or her aides mishandled classified information intentionally or with gross negligence.

As no charges were brought against her, Hillary continues on with her run for president, however the resulting embarrassment is inevitable. Additionally, FBI Director Comey's lecture of Hillary's misconduct gives her opponents another opportunity to criticize her character, honesty, and trustworthiness which have been shown to be her biggest vulnerabilities. However, it seems Comey is still favoring Hillary, since he helped convict a Navy Reservist of mishandling classified materials. Bryan H. Nishimura pleaded guilty to unauthorized removal and retention of classified materials after the FBI found classified information stored in an unauthorized and unclassified system.

Hillary Clinton has numerous classified and top secret documents stored in an unauthorized location. What she did was on a larger scale then what Nishimura did, yet Hillary is not charged. In July of 2015, Nishimura was sentenced to two years of probation and a $7,500 fine. He was also required to surrender all government security clearances. Hillary Clinton has been given security briefings and could soon have the highest security clearance level if elected president. Why is it always that the little guy pays the full price, but Hillary pays no price?

Hillary's constant reiteration through all this is she made a mistake and won't do it again.

Trump rightfully tweeted that adversaries of the U.S. most certainly have a file which they can utilize to possibly blackmail her and this fact alone should now disqualify Hillary from even running for president. He added that the verdict of no charges handed down by the FBI is damning evidence the current political system is rigged, and pointed to Bill's meeting with Lynch in her private plane.
The resulting overall consensus is that Hillary is above the law. The damage done is a terrible precedent that has been set leaving a sour taste in the mouths of U.S. citizens.

A request has been made to the Director of National Intelligence to block Hillary's access to further classified information.

Republican National Committee Chairman Reince Priebus is beside himself regarding the FBI's decision, and deservedly so, stating the clear and gross negligence Hillary demonstrated should have resulted in charges, adding that Hillary Clinton had lied.

The House Select Committee investigation uncovered Hillary's admission that she used her private email server on Benghazi. Theorists believe this may have led to the siege there that killed the four Americans.
She said it was a mistake and that she regrets doing it and would not do that again.

Republican National Convention spokesman Michael Short made a statement that he feels Hillary Clinton is withholding the truth and broke the rules regarding her email server, compromising national security in the process. The only things made clear is her intent to mislead voters by obscuring the facts and her reckless conduct while secretary of state.
The State Department focus has now shifted to whether current employees who were involved in the handling, sending, and receiving of 'Hillary's emails should receive some form of disciplinary action. This could range from a reprimand to the total loss of their security clearance. Former employees found guilty of mishandling classified information could have notes put in their permanent file that could draw consequences

should they seek government employment in the future that would require a security clearance.

House Oversight Committee Chairman Jason Chaffetz stated he will request an FBI probe into whether or not Hillary Clinton lied about her email server to Congress as the consensus is she failed in her role as secretary of state to follow the rules and inform key departmental staff of her actions regarding the use of her private email server.

ENTER ATTORNEY GENERAL LORETTA LYNCH

Chapter 21

The fact is Bill Clinton met with Attorney General Loretta Lynch privately in her jet. Speculation was made he was pleading for Hillary and the email controversy, but there were no witnesses as to what was actually discussed. This meeting was said to be a chance meeting. This is highly unlikely since Loretta and her husband were waiting in their jet for Bill Clinton's plane to land. The meeting was set up to be a secret. The cover story that Clinton and Lynch made up was that they just talked about family.

It must be taken into consideration that Bill appointed Lynch as U.S. Attorney for the Eastern District of New York in 1999—a powerful position overseeing Wall Street and handling cases on some of the most wealthy and influential people in the country.

It was possible Bill Clinton was also pleading for himself as he is an official person of interest in a number of investigations by the Department of Justice. In any event, the meeting was a violation of the Justice Department's policy on communicating with a side in a case, and the rules of impartiality may have been compromised.

There is also the possibility that Bill Clinton was making a deal such that if Attorney General Loretta Lynch did not bring any charges against Hillary Clinton then Hillary Clinton would keep Loretta Lynch as the Attorney General of the United States.

Judical Watch, a conservative organization, has stated "Attorney General Lynch's decision to breach the well-defined ethical standards of the Department of Justice and the American legal pofession is an outrageous abuse of the public's trust." Judicial Watch on June 30, 2016, requested that the U.S. Department of Justice Office of the Inspector General investigate the meeting between Bill Clinton and Attorney General Loretta Lynch.

Max Vanguard

THE CLINTON
FOUNDATION

Chapter 22

The Clinton Foundation is a non-profit corporation under section 501 of the United States tax code. It was founded by Bill Clinton with the mission statement being to "strengthen the capacity of people in the United States and throughout the world to meet the challenges of global interdependence." The website of the organization is clintonfoundation.org. As of September 11, 2016, the website's FAQ page states, "The Bill, Hillary & Chelsea Clinton Foundation builds partnerships between businesses, NGOs, governments, and individuals everywhere to work faster, better, and leaner; to find solutions that last; and to transform lives and communities from what they are today to what they can be tomorrow."

Bill Clinton currently serves as President, and Chelsea Clinton, the daughter of Bill and Hillary, serves as Vice Chair of the Board. The Board is also stacked with former and current Bill and Hillary associates such as Bruce Lindsey and Cheryl Mills, a lawyer and aid to Hillary Clinton.

The Clinton Foundation website states that the foundation helps more than 31,000 American schools with healthy food choices in an effort to eradicate childhood obesity. The website also states that they provide climate-smart agronomic training for higher farmer crop yields in Malawi, Rwanda, and Tanzania.

The Foundation website also states that each year they have reduced 33,500 tons of greenhouse gas emissions in the United States. They state that they are helping with social enterprises in Latin America, the Caribbean, and Asia. They provide people all over the world with CHAI-negotiated prices for HIV/AIDS medications.

In 2014, according to the Clinton Foundation's consolidated statement of financial position, the Foundation took in $112 million in contributions. This is more than double what they reported in 2013. Where did this increase in funding come from? It turns out that much of the money has been raised from foreign individuals.

The New York Times stated the serious nature of having Hillary Clinton run for president of the United States while her husband is raising millions of dollars from foreign individuals. The Washington Post's columnist David Ignatius also found this practice outrageous. He went on to say that wealthy foreign individuals could influence the United States.

MSNBC's Morning Joe reported on Hillary running for president and Bill Clinton collecting funds for the Foundation as "It's just wrong."

Bradley A. Blakeman in a Newsmax.com atricle wrote, "It is clear that there exists probable cause to believe both Hillary and Bill Clinton used a public office (secretary of state and a charity, the Clinton Foundation) in a pay to play scheme of criminal conduct and conspiracy with the aim to provide access and favors from government officials, including but not limited to, the secretary of state in exchange for donations made to the Clinton Foundation, as well as direct payments to Bill Clinton as speaking and consulting fees by individuals (foreign and domestic as well as foreign government officials and states)."

Bernie Sanders, the former democratic challenger to Hillary Clinton has stated on NBC's Meet the Press that Hillary Clinton "should cease all operations, all contact" with the Clinton Foundation if she wins the presidency.

Hillary clearly does not see the issue of Bill Clinton being President of the Foundation while she is president. On September 5, 2016, Hillary Clinton was asked about her husband's role in the Clinton Foundation. Here is what she said: "I don't think there are conflicts of interest," she said in the interview. "I know that that's what has been alleged and never proven. But nevertheless, I take it seriously."

In the same interview Hillary Clinton also stated, "I feel very good about my service as secretary of state. No decision I ever made was influenced by anybody. What I made a decision based on was what was good for the United States, what was good for our values, our interests, and our security. And the State Department has confirmed there's no evidence of any such influence at all."

What is especially troubling about this is if Hillary Clinton believes there is nothing wrong with this now, then clearly a president Clinton would see no issue with funneling billions of dollars wherever she wants. Who would stop her? She would have Loretta Lynch, an already compromised individual caught in the Clinton web as the Attorney General. The congress would be powerless to do anything. They could impeach Hillary in the same way that Bill Clinton was impeached. But the Senate would never convict her. It would simply be labeled a partisan witch hunt and no democrat would vote to convict her. The Obama Administration has seen nothing wrong with sending 400 million dollars in CASH to IRAN which just by pure chance happened on the same day that Iran released captive Americans according to President Barak Obama. With the U.S. government dealing in cash to allegedly work around banking laws that the United States helped set up, one can only imagine what Hillary Clinton would do. There seems to be a clear ethics problem with Hillary's thinking.

In August of 2016, a new batch of emails shows that the U.S. State Department gave special access to a Clinton Foundation donor, Claudio Osorio, while Hillary was Secretary of State. Mr. Osorio received $10 million from the government after the Clinton State Department facilitated the deal from the Overseas Investment Corporation (OPIC) which is a federal agency that operates under the State Department. Mr. Osorio's project was to build houses in Haiti after the 2010 earthquake. The project never broke ground and Osorio used the money to support his millionaire-like lifestyle. Federal prosecutors said that Osorio was sentenced and sent to prison in 2013. The big story here is that a Clinton Foundation donor was given access, which allowed him to secure $10 million for a sham project. Transactions like this make it hard to believe Hillary Clinton when she says, "there's no evidence of any such influence at all."

Bill has been working in the background helping support Hillary's campaign and to build Clinton wealth, by lecturing, writing, and using his influence to get secret donations from sheiks, tycoons, and magnates from around the world. The number and amount of donations quite possibly violates the Memorandum of Understanding (MOU) that limits foreign donations. The Memorandum was an agreement between the Clinton Foundation and the United States government. The memorandum was to limit foreign contributions from foreign governments that wanted to influence the policy of the United States. What is shocking is that if you look at the donors to the Clinton Foundation there are numerous donations from foreign governments.
The Clinton Foundation and the Clinton Health Access Initiative have both ignored New York laws requiring them to disclose the names of foreign

donors. The New York State Attorney General has not attempted to enforce the law. The fact that money is coming into these Clinton organizations from undisclosed foreign individuals hides who could be trying to influence the United States. That said, the Clinton Foundation does list the source of the money, even if they don't name an individual. In many cases it is a corporation, a foundation, or a foreign government. Below is a list of Foundation donors that contributed more than $250,000 since the Foundation was started until the second quarter of 2016.

Greater than $25,000,000
Bill & Melinda Gates Foundation
Clinton Giustra Enterprise Partnership (Canada) *
Fred Eychaner and Alphawood Foundation
Frank Giustra, The Radcliffe Foundation
Nationale Postcode Loterij
The Children's Investment Fund Foundation
UNITAID

$10,000,000 to $25,000,000
AUSAID **
Stephen L. Bing
Commonwealth of Australia ** *
COPRESIDA
Tom Golisano ^
J.B. and M.K. Pritzker Family Foundation *
Kingdom of Norway [Government of Norway] **
Kingdom of Saudi Arabia
Denis J. O'Brien and Digicel *

Cheryl and Haim Saban & The Saban Family Foundation
Susie Tompkins Buell Fund of the Marin Community Foundation
The Elma Foundation
The Hunter Foundation *
The Rockefeller Foundation
The Swedish Postcode Lottery
The Victor Pinchuk Foundation
Theodore W. Waitt

$5,000,001 to $10,000,000
S. Daniel Abraham
Sheikh Mohammed H. Al-Amoudi
C40 Cities Climate Leadership Group, Inc.
Elton John Aids Foundation
Government of the Netherlands **
Irish Aid **
John D. Mackay
Norwegian Agency for Development Cooperation (NORAD) **
OCP Corporation
Michael Schumacher
State of Kuwait
The Clinton Family Foundation
The Coca-Cola Company *
The Wasserman Foundation
Tracfone Wireless, Inc.

$1,000,001 to $5,000,000
100 Women in Hedgefunds
Absolute Return for Kids (ARK)

Acxiom Corporation
Jay Alix
Alliance for a Green Revolution in Africa
Nasser Al-Rashid
American Federation of Teachers *
Angelopoulos Foundation ^
Gianna Angelopoulos ^
Anheuser-Busch Foundation
Smith and Elizabeth Bagley
Banc of California ^ *
Barclays Capital ^
Barclays plc
Mary Bing and Doug Ellis
Bloomberg Philanthropies
Blue Cross and Blue Shield of North Carolina ^
Richard Blum and Blum Family Foundation
BMU - Federal Ministry for the Environment **
Booz Allen Hamilton ^
Carlos Bremer
Richard Caring
Gilbert R. Chagoury
Cheniere Energy, Inc.
Christy and John Mack Foundation
Cisco ^ *
Gustavo Cisneros & Venevision *
Citi Foundation ^
Clinton-Bush Haiti Fund
Stephen J. Cloobeck
Roy E. Cockrum
Victor P. Dahdaleh & The Victor Phillip Dahdaleh
Charitable Foundation
Delos Living ^

Desert Classic Charities Inc
Robert Disbrow
Dubai Foundation
Duke Energy Corporation ^ *
EKTA Foundation
Entergy
Exxonmobil ^
Issam M. Fares
Raj Fernando
Ferraro Family Foundation
Fidelity Charitable Gift Fund
Joseph T. Ford
Wallace W. Fowler
Friends Of Saudi Arabia
Fundacion Telmex
Mala Gaonkar Haarman
GEMS Education

$500,001 to $1,000,000
Abraaj Holdings ^
Akwa Group ^
Alibaba Group
Malini Alles
amfAR: The Foundation for AIDS Research
Andrade Gutierrez S.A. ^
Arizona State University ^
Arkansas Economic Development Commission [Arkansas Energy Office - Arkansas Economic Development] **
Atlas Group Limited
William and Tani Austin
Autodesk, Inc. *

Max Vanguard

Bank of America Foundation
Simón P. Barceló
Barlovento Foundation
Frederick Baron and Lisa Blue
Laurie and Bill Benenson
Arpad Busson
Alonzo Cantu
John and Margo Catsimatidis
Chevron Corporation ^
Citigroup Inc *
Confederaç?o Nacional da Indústria (CNI) ^
Confédération Générale des Entreprises du Maroc
(CGEM) ^
Confederation of Indian Industry ^
Michael J. Cooper
Crabby Beach Foundation
Lewis B. Cullman
Daimler Trucks North America LLC
Dell Inc.
Depart of Finance & Admin. - State Fiscal
Stabilization Fund **
Dozoretz Family Foundation
Emerson Collective *
Energy Developments and Investments
Corporation ^
Foreign Affairs, Trade and Development Canada
(DFATD) **
Fundación Carlos Slim
Matias Garfunkel ^
Gill Foundation
Avram A. and Jill H. Glazer Family
Global Impact *

Jane Goldman
Rolando González Bunster *
Google Inc. *
Brian L. Greenspun
Grupo ABC ^
Hernreich Family Foundation *
Patricia A. Hotung
InterEnergy
Jill and Ken Iscol
Itaú Unibanco S/A ^
J/P Haitian Relief Organization

$250,001 to $500,000
Billye and Henry Aaron *
Accoona Corporation
Abbas I. Al Yousef
Altman/Kazickas Foundation
American Association of University Women ^
American Federation of State, County and Municipal Employees
American International Group, Inc. (AIG) ^
American University in Dubai
Amil Assistłncia Médica Internacional S/A ^
Anim LLC
AstraZeneca Pharmaceuticals LP
James A. Attwood
Farhad Azima
Fred Bacher
Banco Santander Brasil S.A. ^
Barrick Gold Corporation
Anson and Debra Beard
Jack C. Bendheim

BMCE Bank ^
Oliver Bock
Bill Brandt, Patrice Bugelas-Brandt, and Development Specialists, Inc. [Development Specialists, Inc.]
Bright Future International
Susie and Mark Buell
CA Technologies ^ *
Paul L. Cejas
Centene Charitable Foundation
CH2M ^
Channel IT ^
Charles Dunstone Charitable Trust
Charles Stewart Mott Foundation *
City of Little Rock **
Compania De Electricidad De San Pedro De Macoris (Cespm)
Consolidated Contractors Inter. Co. Sal ^
Crédit Agricole du Maroc [Groupe Credit Agricole du Maroc] ^
Beverly Dale *
Martin Davis
Oscar de la Renta
Deutsche Bank AG ^
Deutsche Bank Americas ^
Yongping Duan
Nancy Ellison and William Rollnick
Niko Elmaleh
Embassy of Algeria
Jana and Richard Fant
Morad N. Fareed
Fisher Brothers Foundation, Inc.

Freeport-McMoRan Copper & Gold Foundation ^
Freeport-McMoRan Inc. ^ *
Fuel Freedom Foundation ^
J. B. Fuqua

$250,001 to $500,000
Billye and Henry Aaron *
Accoona Corporation
Abbas I. Al Yousef
Altman/Kazickas Foundation
American Association of University Women ^
American Federation of State, County and Municipal Employees
American International Group, Inc. (AIG) ^
American University in Dubai
Amil Assistlncia Médica Internacional S/A ^
Anim LLC
AstraZeneca Pharmaceuticals LP
James A. Attwood
Farhad Azima
Fred Bacher
Banco Santander Brasil S.A. ^
Barrick Gold Corporation
Anson and Debra Beard
Jack C. Bendheim
BMCE Bank ^
Oliver Bock
Bill Brandt, Patrice Bugelas-Brandt, and Development Specialists, Inc. [Development Specialists, Inc.]
Bright Future International
Susie and Mark Buell

CA Technologies ^ *
Paul L. Cejas
Centene Charitable Foundation
CH2M ^
Channel IT ^
Charles Dunstone Charitable Trust
Charles Stewart Mott Foundation *
City of Little Rock **
Compania De Electricidad De San Pedro De Macoris (Cespm)
Consolidated Contractors Inter. Co. Sal ^
Crédit Agricole du Maroc [Groupe Credit Agricole du Maroc] ^
Beverly Dale *
Martin Davis
Oscar de la Renta
Deutsche Bank AG ^
Deutsche Bank Americas ^
Yongping Duan
Nancy Ellison and William Rollnick
Niko Elmaleh
Embassy of Algeria
Jana and Richard Fant
Morad N. Fareed
Fisher Brothers Foundation, Inc.
Freeport-McMoRan Copper & Gold Foundation ^
Freeport-McMoRan Inc. ^ *
Fuel Freedom Foundation ^
J. B. Fuqua

^ Indicates contributions exclusively for CGI activities such as memberships, sponsorships, and conference fees.
* Indicates a contribution was made by this donor in the second quarter of 2016.

** Indicates government grants.

Max Vanguard

PUTTING IT ALL TOGETHER

Chapter 23

As anyone can plainly see, there are resounding similarities, patterns if you will, between all these scandals that have happened over the last 38 years, which only means two things: Hillary is a compulsive liar only out for her best, self-serving interests, and that she will never stop.

Democratic Presidential Nominee

The next item on her agenda is to be president. Amid the clouds of scandal on her horizon, each move she makes in her career involves higher stakes with regard to power and money. Even if she doesn't win, she will still have made a lot of money in the campaign process.

Just as a leopard cannot change its spots, Hillary has not, cannot, and will not change. She continues to lie and break the rules to maintain her position or get ahead. In the end it's always the same old story.

Regarding her achievements, Hillary's only miraculous accomplishment has been staying out of jail. She has been embroiled in so many investigations through the years that have clearly shown her to be in the wrong, but due to missing evidence or the death of someone who was to testify, has never been charged.

Political pundits are in agreement as to her shortcomings from all the fiascoes over the years and how all of this is negatively impacting her ratings at this crucial time before the fall elections take place.

Hillary Clinton has repeatedly threatened the security of this country by using her personal email server to send and receive classified emails. With regard to the Rose Law Firm billing records case in which records went missing then copies were found, how would that work if she were to become president? A point to be made is that after the files and records go "missing," they somehow then get "found" once Hillary and Bill are cleared.

Obviously her history shows beyond the preponderance of a doubt that there will be more things of greater severity as she seems to be getting more brazen with age.

How can we make decisions based on lies? Lying in a court of law is a crime and punishable. And here we have a lawyer running for the highest office in the land who has repeatedly lied to the country for decades in every position she has held, yet has still been allowed to continue on because of cover-ups, favors called in, and backroom deals.

Choosing Her VP

As far as her Vice President pick of Tim Kaine goes, he really can't help her look honest, and no one votes just for the bottom half of the ticket. She needs him like she needed Bill. He is everything she is not and together they complement each other. They both share the will to fight for progressive causes.

Fall Elections

Before you vote, which I hope you will, take a while to think about the facts, not just the hype and static propaganda generated by the heat of the debates. Ask yourself the proven, strategic questions:

- Has Hillary shown honest consistency putting the needs of the masses before her own throughout her career?

- Who do you trust the most from what they accomplished, not what they said?

- Did you ever trust a person after you found out they lied or deceived you?

- Realize that there are more than two political parties. If you don't like the person running in the Democratic Party, this does not mean that you need to vote for the Republican Party. You can vote for the Libertarian Party, or even the Green Party.

The answers may help to enable you to make a decision you can live with for at least four years.

Armed with this information, many people don't believe Hillary Clinton is fit to be president as demonstrated by her dwindling popularity ratings. With Hillary there is always someone to blame, even if it's her own ignorance. We need capable leaders in these mediocre times. A vote for her is a vote for scandal.

If Hillary Clinton is voted in with her record for the world to see, what will this say about our nation to foreign countries? Are we ready for President Hillary Clinton and First Gentleman Bill? The nations of the world are watching this election closely. If she wins the election, watch out America, they may not view us as rational or intelligent as was once perceived.

CONCLUSION

Max Vanguard

I hope this book was able to help you get a better understanding of the vast number of scandals over many years that Hillary Clinton has been involved in, and the character of the person who is the democratic candidate running in this year's presidential election.

The next step is to approach this material with an open mind before asking yourself if this is the type of scandalous individual you want running our country. Four years can be a long time to wait for another election.

Finally, if you enjoyed this book, please take the time to share your thoughts and post a review on Amazon. It would be greatly appreciated!

Thank you and good luck!

REFERENCES

Watergate, Whitewater, Vince Foster, Cattle Futures, Use of IRS, Chinagate, Lying about Bosnia, Hillary & Women's Rights:
http://www.wnd.com/2015/05/here-they-are-hillarys-22-biggest-scandals-ever/

https://en.wikipedia.org/wiki/Hillary_Rodham_cattle_futures_controversy
http://community.seattletimes.nwsource.com/archive/?date=19940330&slug=1902853

Vince Foster Information:
http://www.dailymail.co.uk/news/article-508210/The-man-knew-The-truth-death-Hillary-Clintons-close-friend-Vince-Foster.html
http://www.wnd.com/2015/05/here-they-are-hillarys-22-biggest-scandals-ever/#!

http://www.thepoliticalinsider.com/new-documents-prove-hillary-clinton-murder-cover/
https://whatyouthoughtiwentaway.wordpress.com/2016/03/02/the-resignation-letter-of-vince-foster/

http://www.wnd.com/2016/02/vince-foster-suicide-shocker-2nd-wound-documented/#!
http://www.liberalforum.org/index.php?/topic/188228-breaking-story-vince-fosters-2nd-wound/

Bill Clinton Indiscretions:
https://en.wikipedia.org/wiki/Bill_Clinton_sexual_misconduct_allegations

http://www.albertpeia.com/oxfordassault.htm
https://www.washingtonpost.com/news/post-politics/wp/2016/03/06/in-an-unusual-allusion-to-bill-clintons-sexual-affair-hillary-clinton-speaks-of-forgiveness/

http://www.refinery29.com/2014/07/71602/hillary-clinton-forgiving-bill-cheating
http://enquirer.com/editions/2003/06/09/tem_monlede09.html

Healthcare Reform 1993:
https://www.boundless.com/u-s-history/textbooks/boundless-u-s-history-textbook/bush-clinton-and-a-changing-world-31/the-clinton-administration-231/the-health-care-plan-of-1993-1317-9290/

Chinagate:
http://www.wnd.com/2015/05/here-they-are-hillarys-22-biggest-scandals-ever/

Ron Brown:
http://www.wnd.com/2013/04/ron-brown-was-hillarys-1st-chris-stevens/#!

http://www.wnd.com/2004/09/26786/#
http://dangerouslogic.com/ron_brown.html

http://www.whatreallyhappened.com/RANCHO/CRASH/BROWN/brown.php#axzz4Jy57i4yN

http://www.whatreallyhappened.com/RANCHO/CRASH/BROWN/bullet.html

Hillary as Secretary of State & Benghazi:
http://www.powerlineblog.com/archives/2016/06/is-hillary-to-blame-for-the-lack-of-a-military-response-in-benghazi.php

http://www.rawstory.com/2016/02/this-is-what-actually-happened-at-the-us-consulate-in-benghazi/

http://www.thepoliticalinsider.com/breaking-smoking-gun-docs-show-hillary-clinton-knew-benghazi-along-whoa/

http://www.judicialwatch.org/press-room/press-releases/judicial-watch-new-benghazi-email-shows-dod-offered-state-department-forces-that-could-move-to-benghazi-immediately-specifics-blacked-out-in-new-document/

Accounting in State Dept.:
https://en.wikipedia.org/wiki/Hillary_Clinton%27s_tenure_as_Secretary_of_State

Women's Rights:
http://www.bloomberg.com/politics/articles/2015-03-10/hillary-clinton-s-long-cautious-record-on-women-s-rights

Superdelegates:
http://www.msnbc.com/msnbc/how-do-superdelegates-work-heres-what-you-need-know

http://www.npr.org/2015/11/13/455812702/clinton-has-45-to-1-superdelegate-advantage-over-sanders

Email Server Scandal:
http://www.independentsentinel.com/attack-scenario-how-hillary-clintons-lust-for-money-and-power-led-to-americas-digital-pearl-harbor/

http://www.cnn.com/2016/07/07/politics/state-department-reopens-probe-into-clinton-emails/index.html

http://www.cnn.com/2016/07/05/politics/fbi-director-doesnt-recommend-charges-against-hillary-clinton/

https://www.fbi.gov/news/pressrel/press-releases/statement-by-fbi-director-james-b.-comey-on-the-investigation-of-secretary-hillary-clintons-use-of-a-personal-e-mail-system
http://www.judicialwatch.org/blog/2016/07/comeys-fbi-helped-convict-navy-reservist-handled-classified-materials-inappropriately/

Loretta Lynch:
http://www.trunews.com/article/did-bill-clinton-cut-a-plea-deal-with-lynch-for-hillary

Verdit, A News Publication from Judicial Watch, September, 2016, Vol. 22, Issue 9

Hillary Lying to Congress:
http://www.newsmax.com/Newsmax-Tv/dick-morris-hillary-clinton-fbi-email/2016/07/07/id/737655/

Foundation:
http://www.newsmax.com/Newsfront/David-Ignatius-Clinton-Foundation-Foreign-Donations-Wrong/2016/08/31/id/746106/

http://www.newsmax.com/BradleyBlakeman/email-foundation/2016/08/30/id/745915/

http://www.newsmax.com/Politics/Sanders-Hillary-Clinton-Foundation-Campaign/2016/09/04/id/746638/

http://www.newsmax.com/Politics/hillary-clinton-foundation-charity/2016/09/06/id/746996/

http://www.newsmax.com/newsfront/daily-caller-clinton-foundation-lied-irs/2016/09/08/id/747318/

http://msnbcmedia.msn.com/i/msnbc/sections/news/understanding.pdf

http://www.judicialwatch.org/blog/2016/08/hillary-state-dept-helped-jailed-clinton-foundation-donor-get-10-mil-u-s-failed-haiti-project/

www.ingramcontent.com/pod-product-compliance
Lightning Source LLC
Chambersburg PA
CBHW070106260726
48658CB00001B/9